# The Mother at Home

# The Mother at Home

John S. C. Abbott

Cedar Lake Classics

# CONTENTS

DEDICATION vii
PREFACE ix

1 Responsibility 1

2 Maternal Authority 17

3 Maternal Authority (Continued) 29

4 The Mother's Difficulties 45

5 Faults and Errors 58

6 Methods and Plans 77

7 Religious Instruction 91

8 Religious Instruction (Continued) 107

9 Fruits of Piety 131

10 Fruits of Piety (Continued) 147

11 Results 164

Copyright © 2022 by Cedar Lake Classics

This is an edited and newly laid out edition of a public domain work.

*TO MY FATHER AND MOTHER*

This book is most affectionately dedicated. For the principles here inculcated, I am indebted to the instructions I received, and the scenes I witnessed, at your fireside. That God may render them available, in conferring the same joy upon other families, which they have so richly shed upon yours, is the prayer of your
*GRATEFUL SON*

# PREFACE

THE MOTHER AT HOME, and its companion and counterpart, the CHILD AT HOME, were written simply with the view of affording to mothers in the common walks of life, plain and simple instruction in respect to the right discharge of their maternal duties, and, at the same time, some practical aid in leading the minds of their children to proper views of their obligations to God, to their parents, and to one another. Although one of the volumes is addressed nominally to the mother, and the other to the child, they are in fact each intended for both mothers and children. If a parent reads and explains the MOTHER AT HOME to her children, they will derive great benefit from the exercise, as they will thus be taught to realize something of the nature and the weight of the responsibilities, the duties, and the cares which such a trust as that which is committed to a mother necessarily brings.

They will thus the more readily acquiesce in the measures adopted for their good, and submit to the authority which ought to be exercised over them; and they may be expected also to imbibe, in some degree, the Christian spirit which the book inculcates. On the other hand, the CHILD AT HOME is intended quite as much to afford to mothers a practical exemplification of the spirit and manner by which their instructions to their children should be characterized, as to act directly upon the children themselves; and its effect even in this last point of view will be greatly enhanced, if the mother, instead of giving her children the book, should read it to them herself, or allow them to read it aloud to her, chapter by chapter, at some calm and silent hour, in the evening or upon the Sabbath, when the hearts of the listeners may be open to salutary impressions, and when the instructions of the printed

## PREFACE

page may be accompanied by the kind and familiar explanations of the living teacher.

The volumes thus, though under different names, aim at one and the same end, and are intended as the counterparts and companions of each other. They regard the family as one—and in explaining and enforcing the relative duties of parents and children, they are intended to exert upon the two classes for which they are designed, a common and simultaneous influence.

Since the original publication of these works, they have been translated into many different languages, and have been circulated very extensively throughout the Christian world. The favor with which they have thus been regarded has led to the republication of them at this time in a new and greatly improved form. The works have been carefully revised, and much enlarged, and the various scenes and incidents described in them are illustrated with numerous engravings, which, it is hoped, will aid in making them attractive both to parents and children.

# 1

# Responsibility

A FEW years ago, some gentlemen who were associated together in a religious institution, in a course of preparation for the Christian ministry, conceived the design of ascertaining what proportion of their number were the children of pious mothers. They were greatly surprised and greatly pleased at finding that out of one hundred and twenty students, over one hundred had been borne by a mother's prayers, and directed by a mother's counsels, to the Savior.

Though some of these had in early life broken away from the restraints of home, and like the prodigal, had wandered deviously for a time in paths of sin and sorrow, yet they could not even in their wanderings forget the impressions of childhood, and were eventually brought to the Savior, in fulfillment of the promises made so frequently in the Scriptures, that success shall sooner or later attend the efforts of parental fidelity, faith, and prayer. Many other striking examples might be added, in addition to this, to show how intimate is the connection between the Christian character of the mother and the salvation of the child.

The efforts which a mother makes for the improvement of her children in knowledge and virtue are necessarily retired and unobtrusive. The world knows not of them; and hence the world has been slow to perceive how powerful and extensive is this secret and silent influence. But circumstances are now directing the eyes of the community to the young, and the truth is daily coming more distinctly into view, that the influence which is exerted upon the mind during the first eight or ten years of existence, in a great degree guides the destinies of that mind for time and eternity. And as the mother is the guardian and guide of the early years of life, from her emanates the most powerful influence which is exerted in the formation of the character of man. And why should it not be so? What impressions can be stronger, and more lasting, than those received upon the mind in the freshness and the susceptibility of youth? What instructor can gain greater confidence and respect than a mother? And where can there exist circumstances more favorable for guiding human souls into the way of salvation, than when the little flock cluster around a mother's knee to hear of God and heaven?

"A good boy generally makes a good man." Said the mother of Washington, "George was always a good boy." It was this always having been a good boy in childhood that constitutes one great secret of the subsequent greatness of Washington. He had a mother who made him a good boy and instilled into his heart those principles which raised him to be the benefactor of his country, and one of the brightest ornaments of the world. The mother of Washington is entitled to a nation's gratitude. She taught her boy the principles of obedience, and moral courage, and virtue. She, in a great measure, formed the character of the hero, and the statesman. It was by her own fireside that she taught her boy in the playful years of infancy, to govern himself; and it was thus that he was prepared for the brilliant career of usefulness which he afterward pursued. We are indebted to God for the gift of Washington; but we are no less indebted to him for the gift of his inestimable mother. Had she been a weak, and indulgent, and unfaithful parent, the unchecked energies of her son might have elevated him to the throne of a tyrant; or youthful disobedience might have prepared the way for a life of crime and a dishonored grave.

Byron had a mother just the reverse of lady Washington; and we see the character of the mother in this case also, reflected in that of the son. We cannot wonder at the character and conduct of Byron, for we see them to be the almost necessary consequence of the education which he received, and the scenes which he witnessed in his mother's parlor. She would at one time allow him to disobey with impunity; at another she would fly into a rage and beat him. She thus taught him to defy all authority, human and divine; to indulge, without restraint, in sin; to give himself up to the power of every maddening passion. It was the mother of Byron who laid the foundation of his pre-eminence in guilt. She taught him to plunge into that sea of profligacy and wretchedness, upon whose agitated waves he was tossed for life. If the crimes of the poet deserve the execration of the world—the world cannot forget that it was the mother who fostered in his youthful heart those passions which made the son a curse to his fellowmen.

There are, it is true, innumerable causes incessantly operating in the formation of character. A mother's influence is by no means the only influence which is exerted. Still, it may be the most powerful; for, with God's ordinary blessing, it may form in the youthful mind the habits, and implant the principles, to which other influences are to give permanency and vigor.

A pious and faithful mother may have a dissolute child. Her son may break away from all restraints, and God may leave him to "eat the fruit of his own devices." The parent, thus afflicted and broken-hearted, can only bow before the sovereignty of her Maker, who says, "be still, and know that I am God." The consciousness, however, of having done one's duty, divests this affliction of much of its bitterness. And besides, such cases are rare. Profligate children are generally the offspring of parents who have neglected the moral and religious education of their family. Some parents are themselves profligate, and thus not only allow their children to grow up unrestrained, but by their example lure them to sin. But there are others who are very upright, and virtuous, and even pious themselves, who do nevertheless, neglect the moral culture of their children; and as a consequence, they grow up in disobedience and sin. It matters but little what the cause is which leads to this neglect. The neglect itself will ordinarily be followed by disobedience and self-will.

Hence the reason that children of eminent men, both in church and state, are not infrequently the disgrace of their parents. If the mother is unaccustomed to govern her children, if she looks wholly to the father to enforce obedience from them, and control them; when he is absent, all family government is absent, and the children are left to run wild; to learn lessons of disobedience; to practice arts of deception; to build, upon the foundation of contempt for a mother, a character of insubordination and iniquity. But if the children are under the efficient government of a judicious mother, the reverse of this is almost invariably the case. And since, in nearly every instance, the early years of life are entrusted to a mother's care, it follows that maternal influence, more than anything else, forms the future character.

The history of John Newton is often adduced as a proof of the deep and lasting impression which a mother may produce upon the mind of her child. He had a pious mother. She often retired with him to her closet, and placing her hand upon his youthful head, implored God's blessing upon her boy. These prayers and instructions sank deep into his heart. He could not but revere that mother. He could not but feel that there was a holiness in such a character, demanding reverence and love. He could not tear from his heart, in after-life, the impressions then produced. Though he became a wicked wanderer, though he forsook friends and home, and every virtue—yet the remembrance of a mother's prayers, like a guardian-angel, followed him wherever he went.

He mingled in the most dissipated and disgraceful scenes of a sailor's life, and while surrounded with guilty associates, in midnight revelry, he would fancy he felt the soft hand of his mother upon his head, pleading with God to forgive and bless her boy. He went to the coast of Africa and became even more degraded than the savages upon her dreary shores. But the soft hand of his mother was still upon his head, and the fervent prayers of his mother still thrilled in his heart. And this influence, after the lapse of many guilty years, brought back the prodigal, a penitent and a child of God; elevated him to be one of the brightest ornaments of the Christian church, and enabled him to guide many sons and daughters to glory. What a forcible comment is this upon the power of maternal influence! And what encouragement does this present to every mother to be faithful in her efforts to train up her child for God! Had Mrs. Newton neglected her duty, had she even been as remiss as many Christian mothers are, her son, to all human view, might have continued in sin, and been an outcast from heaven. It was through the influence of the mother that the son was saved. Newton became afterward a most successful preacher of the gospel, and every soul that he was instrumental in saving, in singing the song of redeeming mercy, will, through eternity, bless God that Newton had such a mother.

The influence thus exerted upon the mind, in early childhood, may, for many years, be apparently lost. When a son leaves home, and enters upon the busy world, many are the temptations which come crowding upon him. If when he thus withdraws from his mother's personal watch and care, his heart has not been fortified with established principles of religion and of self-control, he will most assuredly fall before these temptations. He may indeed fall, even after all that a mother has done, or can do; and he may become deeply involved in guilt. But even then, when he has apparently forgotten every lesson that he learned at home, the secret influence of a mother's instructions, and a mother's prayers, may be yet working powerfully and effectually in his heart. He will think of a mother's tears, when remorse keeps him awake at midnight, or when danger threatens him with speedy arraignment at the bar of God. The thoughts of the sacredness of home will often throw bitterness into his cup of guilty pleasure and compel him to sigh for the virtue and the peace which he has forsaken. Even though far away, in abodes of infamy, degraded and abandoned, he must occasionally think of a broken-hearted mother. Thus, may he, after many years, perhaps long after she has gone down to the grave, be led, by the remembrance of her virtues, to forsake his sins.

A short time since, a gentleman, in one of our most populous cities, was going to attend a seaman's meeting in the mariner's chapel. Directly opposite to the chapel there was a sailor's boarding-house. In the doorway of this house there was a hardy, weather-beaten sailor, sitting with arms folded, and smoking a cigar—watching the people as they gradually assembled for the meeting.

The gentleman walked up to him and said, "Well, my friend, won't you go with us to meeting?"

"No!" said the sailor, bluntly.

The gentleman, who, from the appearance of the man, had been prepared for a repulse, mildly replied, "You look, my friend, as though you had seen hard days; have you a mother?" The sailor raised his head, looked earnestly in the gentleman's face, and made no reply.

The gentleman continued: "Suppose your mother were here now, what advice do you think that she would give you?" The tears rushed into the eyes of the poor sailor; he endeavored for a moment to conceal them but could not; and hastily brushing them away with the back of his rough hand, rose and said with a voice almost inarticulate through emotion, "I'll go to the meeting." He crossed the street, entered the door of the chapel, and took his seat with the assembled congregation. What afterward became of the man is not known. It is however almost certain that he must have had a mother who had given him good instruction; and when the gentleman appealed to her, hardened as the sailor was, his heart melted. It is by no means improbable that this interview may have checked this man in his sins and led him to Christ. At any event, it shows the strength of maternal influence. It shows that years of wandering and of sin cannot erase from the heart the impression which a mother's instructions and a mother's prayers have left there.

It is a great trial to have children undutiful when young; but it is a tenfold greater affliction to have a child grow up to maturity in disobedience and become a dissolute and abandoned man. How many parents have passed days of sorrow and nights of sleeplessness in consequence of the misconduct of their offspring! How many have had their hearts broken, and their gray hairs brought down with sorrow to the grave, solely in consequence of their own neglect to train up their children in the nurture and admonition of the Lord! Your future happiness is in the hands of your children. They may be the means of filling all the future years of your life with joy, and on the other hand they may throw gloom over all your prospects, embitter every enjoyment, and make you so miserable, that your only prospect of relief will be in death.

That little girl whom you tenderly hold upon your knee, and who plays, so full of enjoyment, upon your floor, has entered a world where temptations are thick around. What is to enable her to resist these temptations, but established principles of piety? And where is she to obtain these principles, but from a mother's instructions and example? If, through your neglect now, she should hereafter yield herself to temptation and sin, what must become of your peace of mind? O mother! Little are you aware of the wretchedness with which your loved daughter may hereafter overwhelm you!

Many illustrations of the most affecting nature might be here introduced. It would be easy to appeal to a vast number of living sufferers, in attestation of the woe which the sin of a child can occasion. You may go, not only in imagination, but in reality, to the darkened chamber where the mother sits weeping, and refusing to be comforted, for a daughter lost to virtue and to heaven. Still, though we may wit- ness the scene, no one but those who have experienced it can conceive how overwhelming is the mental agony which must prey upon a mother thus dishonored and broken-hearted. This is a sorrow which can only be understood by one who has tasted its bitterness and felt its weight. We may go to the house of piety and prayer and find the father and mother with countenances emaciated with suffering; not a smile plays upon their features, and the mournful accents of their voice tell how deeply seated is their sorrow. Shall we inquire into the cause of this heart-rending grief? The mother would only reply with tears and sobs. The father would summon all his fortitude, and say, "my daughter"—and say no more. The anguish of his spirit would prevent the further utterance of his grief.

Is this exaggeration? No! Let your lovely daughter, now your pride and joy, be abandoned to infamy, be an outcast from society, and you must feel what language cannot express.

This is a dreadful subject; but the danger is one which the mother ought to feel and understand. None are exempt from it. There are facts which might here be introduced, sufficient to make every parent tremble. We might lead you to the dwelling of the clergyman and tell you that a daughter's sin has carried the mother to the grave, and sent paleness to the cheek, and trembling to the frame, and agony to the heart of the aged father. We might carry you to the parlor of the rich man, and show you all the elegance and the opulence with which he is surrounded; and yet he would tell you that he was one of the most unhappy of the sons of affliction, and that he would gladly give all his treasures if he could purchase back a daughter's virtue; that he could gladly lie down to die, if he could by so doing, even blot out the remembrance of a daughter's infamy.

No matter what your situation in life may be, that little child, now so innocent, whose playful endearments and happy laugh awaken such thrilling emotions in your heart, may cause you years of most unalleviated misery.

And mother! Look at that drunken vagrant, staggering by your door. Listen to his horrid imprecations, as bloated and ragged he passes along. That wretch has a mother. Perhaps, widowed and in poverty, she needs the comfort and support of an affectionate son. You have a son. You may soon be a widow. In that case if your son is dissolute, you are doubly widowed; you are worse, infinitely worse than childless. You cannot now endure even the thought that your son will ever be thus abandoned. How dreadful then must be the experience of the reality! I once knew a mother who had an only son. She loved him most ardently and could not bear to deny him any indulgence. He, of course, soon learned to rule his mother. At the death of his father, the poor woman was left at the mercy of this vile boy. She had neglected her duty when he was young, and now his ungovernable passions had become too strong for her control. Self-willed, turbulent, and revengeful, he was his mother's bitterest curse. His paroxysms of rage at times amounted almost to madness. One day, infuriated against his mother, he set fire to her house, and it was burned to the ground, with all its contents, and she was left in the extreme of poverty. He was imprisoned as an incendiary, and, in his cell, he became a maniac, if he was not such before, and madly dug out his own eyes. He now lies in perpetual darkness, confined by the stone walls and grated bars of his dungeon, an infuriated madman.

How hard it must be for a mother, after all her anxiety, and suffering —her days of toil, and her nights of watching and care, to find her son a demoniac enemy, instead of a guardian and friend! You have watched over your child, through all the months of its helpless infancy. You have denied yourself, that you might give it comfort. When it has been sick, you have been unmindful of your own weariness, and your own weakness, and the livelong night you have watched at its cradle, administering to all its wants. When it has smiled, you have felt a joy which none but a parent can feel, and have pressed your much-loved treasure to your bosom, praying that its future years of obedience and affection might be your ample reward. And now, how dreadful a requital, for that child to grow up to hate and abuse you; to leave you friendless, in sickness and in poverty; to squander all his earnings in haunts of iniquity and degradation.

There is, in many families, an impression that the boys must soon grow beyond a mother's control or influence, and that, while it is expected that the girls should still be obedient to their mother, the sons must, at a certain age, be left to the control of the father. Thus, insensibly they imbibe the feeling that they are above their mother's authority. The mother feels that she has no power to govern them; the father is away, and the whole mind is engrossed with other cares, and the boys are left uncontrolled. This is the influential cause of the ruin of thousands of families.

Probably there is not one who will read this page, who cannot recall to mind many illustrations of the truth of this statement. Here is a lost son dying in the forecastle of a ship, far away upon the ocean. Why is he there, far from his own pleasant fireside and the love of home? Because his mother never established any control over her boy. In his infancy she indulged him, under the influence of an overwhelming maternal fondness. The injury might possibly have been retrieved in the early years of boyhood, but the golden opportunity was allowed to slip by. The boy, as he grew in strength and energy, became reck- less and uncontrollable, and after a long and sorrowful experience of struggle, disappointment, and suffering, he was sent to sea, to perish miserably in some noxious foreign clime.

Here is a mutilated corpse upon some bloodstained field of battle. The form is that of a graceful youth, whose fair cheek is hardly browned by the southern sun. Why has this young man been plunged into these awful scenes of human butchery, and come to this untimely and disgraceful death? It is because his mother did not control him when he was a child.

The idea is a totally erroneous one, that a son, by nature, feels that there is an inferiority in a woman, and that it is not manly to obey his mother. The natural feeling is just the reverse, and a judicious mother can retain control over a son as long as he lives. The bond will be changed it is true, when he becomes a man, from that of authority to that of affection, but it will endure to the end of life, and grow stronger and stronger every year.

Indeed, a well-educated young man feels a peculiar pride in being obedient to his mother. There is a chivalrous feeling, a sense of honor connected with such submission which is highly pleasurable to every ingenuous mind.

No one can read the biography of Payson without seeing the control which a mother's mind exerted over him, through all his collegiate and theological course, and when all the cares of his arduous profession were crowding him. The same maternal supremacy which protected his infancy, guided and curbed the impetuosity of his childhood, the ardor of his youth, and the energies of his manhood. For the mother may be, in many things, always the superior of her son, and be capable of being his counselor and benefactor.

The memoirs of Wesley, who has, perhaps, exerted as powerful an influence as any other man upon the destinies of the world, are filled with illustrations of this continued influence of a mother's mind guiding her apostolical son in all the conflicts of his laborious and glorious career.

Read the letters of the mother of John Quincy Adams, and you will be at no loss to account for the invincible moral courage, the unvarying principle, and the almost superhuman energy which has shed such luster upon his life. Before her noble mind he was ever proud to bow in homage. He was always, even in the most exalted manhood, his mother's child, ever prompt to do her bidding, and ever feeling himself honored in honoring her.

Even the Emperor Napoleon attributed the formation of his character, in a great measure, to his mother's influence. And in speaking on the subject generally, he remarked, that "the man is what the mother makes him. France wants mothers."

In fact, every young man wants to be proud of his mother. He loves to feel under her control. He delights in having a mother who is capable and worthy of guiding him. And she who virtually abandons the government of her boy just as he is entering upon the fiery temptations of impetuous youth, inflicts upon him an irreparable injury, and is an almost unpardonable betrayer of her sacred trust.

From these and similar facts it is plain that God has placed in the hands of parents an influence which is almost boundless. We are very prone to underrate this power. You observe that your child has some fault which you endeavor to remove. Persuasion, entreaty, punishment —all perhaps fail, or secure only partial success; and you say, "How little influence have I, after all, over my child." But you forget that there is an influence of conduct and example as well as of precept, and that very probably, by your own previous neglect or sin, you may yourself have riveted the chain which you now strive in vain to break by a word.

Besides the individual instances that have been adduced, we can see the influence to parents by observing how national characteristics are preserved from generation to generation. The population of Turkey, of

China, of New England, and of every savage island, will in one hundred years be slumbering in the ground, and their places will be filled by others, who will all be substantially alike when they enter the world. The millions of infants who are to compose the next Turkish generation will not, as infants, differ from those who are to be our descendants in this happy land—or from the future throng which will fill the Chinese empire—or from the babes which open their eyes in the wildest hut or wigwam. And yet how certainly will every one of these classes, as they come forward into life, receive the traits of mind and the characteristics of their parents. How certainly will the next generation in Turkey be substantially like the last, and China in the twentieth century be like China now, unless some extraneous cause comes in to produce a change. The power of parental influence is almost unbounded.

But besides the influence which mothers can thus exert in securing the future welfare and happiness of their children, their own enjoyment, in their declining years, is almost wholly dependent upon the results of their dealings with those thus dependent upon them. The influence which you now exert upon your children will react, after many years, with prodigious power upon yourselves. It is natural that in early life parents should have no conception of the extent to which their own peace and happiness are ultimately to be placed in their children's hands. See that infant: weakness and helplessness itself, it has scarcely strength to sustain its own tottering footsteps, or courage to look without agitation into a stranger's face; dependent for every want, and completely submissive to every command, it can scarcely be said to have a separate existence. It knows nothing— it does nothing, but through parental permission; and if there is throughout the world an instance of complete, unlimited, absolute power on the one hand, and most entire and helpless submission on the other, it is to be found in the empire which such a parent holds over such a child.

We see very clearly in such a case how entirely the happiness of the child is dependent upon the mother, but it is hard to realize how soon the state of the case will be reversed, and the mother become equally dependent for all her happiness upon the child.

Difficult as it is, however, to realize this, it is nevertheless true.

The child advances with an irresistible progress up through the years of childhood and youth; and as it passes on from year to year, the bonds of this dependence and helplessness melt gradually away. You cannot stop the progress of years; you cannot check the advance to maturity; the mind of your child will expand beyond your grasp; the powers of the being, once so helpless, will rise slowly, but irresistibly above your own control; and he will, ere you are aware, stand forth mature, independent, and free—to carry forward with an impetus which you might once have guided, but which now you cannot stop, his course of happiness or suffering; to bring down upon your own head the blessings or the curses which you have taught him to procure.

It must be remembered, too, that the bonds by which you are bound to your children— and through which any fidelity or unfaithfulness which you may now exhibit will return with tenfold power upon your own head in future years—you can never sunder. You cannot, should you ever desire to do it, banish affection from your heart. You cannot say, when hereafter he comes to a course of sin and suffering, "I will leave him to his own chosen way and be myself indifferent about his joys and sorrows."

No; the cord which binds you to him is too strong. God has fastened it; and the more his wayward propensities may pull upon the knot, the tighter it will be drawn. Even his death will not sunder it. You will linger over his grave, and busy memory will bring back to you the long-passed scenes through which you may have accompanied him. The neglected duty will come up again to view; the indulgence which ought to have been denied will reproach; the recollections of unfaith- fulness will sting; and, on the other hand, the severity of affliction will be assuaged by the remembrance of all your sincere and earnest efforts to do your duty, and to prepare your departed child for heaven. You will be excited to fidelity in duty "by looking forward frequently to your approaching separation from your children." The ties which bind you, however closely, to them, must soon be sundered by death. You must, before many years, see them deposited in the grave, or you must bid them farewell, while they stand weeping around your own dying bed. They may be summoned first; and you will find, as every bereaved parent well knows, that mourning for their loss is the bitterest cup of sorrow which you can drink. You may have wept for other friends before; you may have followed your own beloved parents to the grave; but, in the emphatic language of an afflicted father, you will find "parental anguish more deep and keen than filial." At such an hour you will need consolation; and nothing will have greater power to assuage your sorrow, than the recollections of your past fidelity, in training up your child for heaven.

If these efforts have been made, and have been attended by the ordinary blessing of God, your child may give evidence at a very early age of his affection for his Savior, and of his preparation for another world.

But although you may survive your children, they will probably survive you. You will have to leave them in a world of temptation and danger, with no sufficient protector, unless you can have secured for them the protection of a friend above. When your last hours are passing, and the world begins to recede from view, its various ties will, one after another, be surrendered, and broken: but, after all others are gone, the bond which connects you with your child will still cling. That link will be the last to be severed; so that when you are willing and desirous to leave everything else that is earthly, your heart will still linger about your fireside, and affection for a beloved child will make you cling to life. How happy will it be for you at such a time, to feel that God will be a parent to the orphans—and that you separate from them only for a time. If your faithful instructions have instilled the principles of piety into their hearts, you can have this happiness; and you can with peaceful resignation commit them to God's care, assured that he will be their supporter in the temptations of life, and their refuge in its storms.

Let these thoughts dwell with you to encourage and to strengthen you in your present duties. While you are making strenuous and faithful efforts to improve the character and strengthen the moral and religious principles of your child, be encouraged by the assurance, that long after these struggles shall be over, you will think of them and dwell upon them with pleasure. On the other hand, remember, that if you set it an example of sin, or act in your management under the influence of indolence or irritation, consulting present convenience, without attempting to follow any fixed principles—oh, remember, that though an act of unfaithfulness may be over in an hour, its memory will last, and it will bite like a serpent, and sting like an adder.

How entirely thus is your earthly happiness at the disposal of your child! His character is now, in an important sense, in your hands, and you are to form it for good or for evil. If you are consistent in your government, and faithful in the discharge of your duties, your child will probably through life revere you, and be the stay and solace of your declining years. If, on the other hand, you cannot summon resolution to punish your child when disobedient; if you do not curb his passions; if you do not bring him to entire and willing subjection to your authority; you must expect that he will be your curse. In all probability, he will despise you for your weakness. Unaccustomed to restraints at home, he will break away from all restraints, and make you wretched by his life, and disgraceful in his death.

But few parents think of this as they ought. They are not conscious of the momentous consequences which depend upon the efficient and decisive government of their children. Thousands of parents now stand in our land like oaks blighted and scathed by lightnings and storms. Thousands have had every hope wrecked, every prospect darkened, and have become the victims of the most agonizing and heart-rending disappointment, solely in consequence of the misconduct of their children. And yet thousands of others are going on in the same way, preparing to experience the same suffering, and are apparently un- conscious of their danger.

Such are the responsibilities of mothers. How few parents there are that fully realize the weight and importance which they assume, when we calmly consider them.

It is true that there are many mothers who feel their responsibilities perhaps as deeply as it is best they should feel them. But there are many others—even Christian mothers—who seem to forget that their children will ever be less under their control than they are while young. And they are training them up, by indecision and indulgence, soon to tyrannize over their parents with a rod of iron—and to pierce their hearts with many sorrows. If you are unfaithful to your child when he is young, he will be unfaithful to you when he is old. If you indulge him in all his foolish and unreasonable wishes when he is a child, when he becomes a man he will indulge himself; he will gratify every desire of his heart; and your sufferings will be rendered the more poignant by the reflection that it was your own unfaithfulness which has caused your ruin. If then you would be the happy mother of a happy child, give your attention, and your efforts, and your prayers, to the great duty of training him up for God and heaven.

# 2

# Maternal Authority

IN the preceding chapter I have endeavored to show the mother how much her happiness is dependent upon the good or bad character of her children. Your own reflections and observations have, doubtless, impressed this subject most deeply upon your heart. The question has probably often presented itself to your mind, while reading the previous chapter, "How shall I govern my children, so as to secure their virtue and happiness?" This question I shall now endeavor to answer.

## Obedience Essential

Obedience is absolutely essential to proper family Without this, all other efforts will be in vain. You may pray with, and for your children; you may strive to instruct them in religious truth; you may be unwearied in your efforts to make them happy, and to gain their affection; but if they grow up in habits of disobedience, your instructions will be lost, and your toil will all be in vain. And by obedience, I do not mean languid and dilatory yielding to repeated threats, but prompt and cheerful acquiescence in the parental will. Neither is it enough that a child should yield to your arguments and persuasions. It is essential that he should submit to your authority.

I will suppose a case in illustration of this last remark. Your little daughter is sick; you go to her with the medicine which has been prescribed for her, and the following dialogue ensues.

"Here, my daughter, is some medicine for you." "I don't want to take it, mamma."

"Yes, my child, do take it, for it will make you better." "No, it will not, mother; I don't want it."

"Yes, it will, my child; the doctor says it will."

"Well, it isn't good, and I don't want it." The mother continues her persuasions, and the child persists in its refusal. After a long and wearisome conflict, the mother is compelled either to throw the medicine away, or to resort to compulsion, and force down the unpalatable drug. Thus, instead of appealing at once to her own supreme authority, she enters into a long and useless controversy with the reason of the child, under circumstances in which the child of course refuses to be convinced.

A mother, once, under similar circumstances, not being able to persuade her child to take the medicine, and not having sufficient resolution to compel it to do so, threw the medicine away. When the physician next called, she was ashamed to acknowledge her want of power over her child, and therefore did not tell him that the medicine had not been taken. The physician finding the patient worse, left another prescription, supposing that the previous one had been properly administered. But the child could no more be convinced of the necessity of taking the nauseous dose, in the second instance than in the first, and all the efforts of the mother were unavailing.

Again the fond and foolish, but cruel parent, threw the medicine away, and the fever was left to rage unchecked in the patient's veins. Again the physician called, and was surprised to find how inefficacious his prescriptions were; and to perceive that the poor little sufferer was at the verge of death. The mother, when informed that her child must die, was in an agony, and confessed what she had done. But it was too late. The child died. And think you that mother gazed upon its pale corpse with any common emotions of anguish? Think you that the idea never entered her mind that she was the destroyer of her child?

Physicians will tell you that many children have been thus lost. Unaccustomed to obedience when well, they were still more averse to it when sick. Then there is another danger besides. The efforts which are made to induce a stubborn child to take medicine, often produce such an excitement as entirely to counteract the effect of the prescription; and thus is a mother often called to weep over the grave of her child, simply because she has not taught that child to obey.

It is certainly the duty of parents sometimes to explain to their children the reasonableness and propriety of their requirements. This should be done to instruct them, and to make them acquainted with moral obligation. But there should always be authority sufficient to enforce prompt obedience, whether the child can see the reason of the requirement or not. Indeed, it is impossible to govern a child by mere argument. Many cases must occur, in which it will be incapable of seeing the reasonableness of the command; and often its wishes will be so strongly opposed to duty, that all the efforts to convince its understanding will be in vain. The first thing therefore to be aimed at in the training of your child, is to bring him under perfect subjection to your will. Teach him that he must obey you. Sometimes give him your reasons; at other times withhold them. But let him perfectly understand that whether reasons are given or not, he is to do whatever you require.

Accustom him to immediate and cheerful acquiescence in your will. This is obedience. And this is absolutely essential to good family government. Without this, your family will present one continued scene of noise and confusion; the toil of rearing up your children will be almost insupportable, and, in all probability, your heart will be broken by their future ingratitude, and perhaps open sin. To illustrate more fully my meaning in the remark, that it is not always best to give reasons to children, let me suppose a case. A boy comes to his mother for permission to go out into the street to play during the evening.

"No, my child," says the mother, "I would rather that you should not go. They are bad boys, and you will learn bad habits. I think you had better stay in."

"But, mother, I do not think they are bad boys. William and John are there, and I don't see why I cannot go."

"They use bad language, and are rude. Besides, it is cold, and I don't think it would be pleasant for you tonight. I think you will be much happier if you stay in with us."

"Why, mother, if they use bad language I will come away. They are going to have a fine game, and I want to go very much."

Thus there is a protracted discussion which probably ends in the victory of the boy. The mother does not perceive that all her arguments are entirely nullified by the boy's strong desire for the indulgence. That completely intoxicates him. It is perfectly idle, at such a time, to attempt to convince him. He is blinded completely; and the only proper course is to say mildly, but firmly, "No, my child, you must not go." "Why not, mother? I want to go."

"I cannot tell you why not, now. I will talk with you about it another time." Then let the mother wait until her son has spent some evening happily at home, and just before he retires to rest, while his conscience is at peace— and his mind pre-disposed in favor of domestic duty and happiness—let her point out to him the reason why she keeps him from the streets and from the rude and noisy scenes of temptation and sin, that are presented there.

Let all similar requests for sinful or dangerous indulgences always be decided by authority, and not by persuasion, unless, as was suggested above, you may sometimes wish to leave your child to decide for himself, that he may learn wisdom from experience. This, however, ought to be done very seldom, and with great caution; or else you will find that while you were endeavoring to disgust him with the evils of sin, you will have been hardening his conscience against its guilt.

## How Obedience is Established

We come now to the inquiry, how is the habit of obedience to be established? This is not so difficult a matter as many imagine. It does not require profound learning, or any mysterious skill pertaining but to the Where do you find the best regulated families? Are they in the houses of the rich? Do the children of our most eminent men furnish the best patterns for imitation? Obviously not. In some of the most humble dwellings we find the beautiful spectacle of an orderly and well-regulated family. On the other hand, in the mansions of the wealthiest or most eminent men of our country, we may often find a family of rude girls and ungovernable boys—a picture of wild misrule. It is not greatness of talent, or profound learning, which is requisite to teach a child obedience. The principles by which we are to be guided are very simple and very plain.

Never give a command which you do not intend shall be obeyed. There is no more effectual way of teaching a child disobedience, than by giving commands which you have no intention of enforcing. A child is thus habituated to disregard its mother; and in a short time the habit becomes so strong, and the child's contempt for the mother so confirmed, that entreaties and threats are alike unheeded.

"Mary! Mary! you must not touch the book," says a mother to her little daughter, who is attempting to pull the Bible from the table. Mary stops for a moment, and then takes hold of the book again.

Pretty soon the mother looks up and sees that Mary is still playing with the Bible. "Did not you hear me tell you that you must not touch the book?" she exclaims: "why don't you obey?"

Mary takes away her hand for a moment, but is soon again at her forbidden amusement. By and by, down falls the Bible upon the floor. The mother rises in anger, and hastily gives the child a passionate blow, exclaiming, "There! The next time obey me." The child falls upon the floor and fills the apartment with cries of resentment and anger, while the mother replaces the fallen volume, wondering why it is that her children do not obey her commands.

This is not a very agreeable family scene, but everyone of my readers will admit that it is not an uncommon one. And is it strange that a child, thus managed, should be disobedient? No. She is actually led on by her mother to insubordination; she is actually taught to pay no heed to parental injunctions. Even the improper punishment which sometimes follows transgression, is not inflicted on account of the disobedience of the child, but for the accidental consequences which result from it. In the case above described, had the Bible not fallen, the disobedience of the child would have passed unpunished.

I was once, when riding in the country, overtaken by a shower, and compelled to seek shelter in a farmhouse. Half a dozen rude and ungovernable boys were racing about the room, in such an uproar as to prevent the possibility of conversation with the father, who was sitting by the fire. As I, however, endeavored to make some remark, the father shouted out, "Stop that noise, boys."

They paid no more heed to him than they did to the rain. Soon again, in an irritated voice, he exclaimed, "Boys, be still, or I will whip you: as sure as you are alive I will." But the boys, as though accustomed to such threats, screamed and quarreled on without intermission.

At last the father said to me, " I believe 1 have got the worst boys in town; I never can make them mind me."

The fact was, these boys had the worst father in town. He was teaching them disobedience as directly and efficiently as he could. He was giving commands which he had no intention of enforcing, and they knew it. This, to be sure, is an extreme case. But just so far as any mother allows her authority to be disregarded, so far does she expose herself to the contempt of her children, and actually teaches them lessons of disobedience.

And is there any difficulty in enforcing obedience to any definite command? Take the case of the child playing with the Bible. A mild and judicious mother says distinctly and decidedly to her child, "My daughter, that is not a book for you, and you must not touch it." The child hesitates for a moment, but yielding to the strong temptation, is soon playing with the forbidden book. The mother immediately rises, takes the child, and carries her into her chamber. She sits down and says calmly, "Mary, I said that you must not touch the Bible, and you have disobeyed me. I am very sorry, for now I must punish you."

Mary begins to cry, and to promise not to do so again.

"But, Mary," says the mother, "you have disobeyed me, and you must be punished."

Mary continues to cry, but the mother seriously and calmly punishes her. She inflicts real pain—pain that will be remembered.

She then says, " Mary, it makes me unhappy to punish you. I love my little daughter, and wish to have her a good girl."

She then perhaps leaves her to herself for a few minutes. A little solitude will deepen the impression made.

In five or ten minutes she returns, takes Mary in her arms and says, " Mary, are you sorry that you disobeyed me?" Almost any child would answer "Yes."

"Will you be careful and not disobey me again?" "Yes, mother."

"Well, Mary," says her mother, "I will forgive you, so far as I can; but God is displeased; you have disobeyed him as well as me. Do you wish me to ask God to forgive you?"

"Yes, mother," answers the child.

The mother then kneels with her daughter and offers a simple prayer for forgiveness, and for the return of peace and happiness. She then leads her out, humbled and subdued. At night, just before she goes to sleep, she mildly and affectionately reminds her of her disobedience, and advises her to ask God's forgiveness again. Mary, in child-like simplicity, acknowledges to God what she has done, and asks him to forgive her, and take care of her, during the night.

When this child awakes in the morning, will not her young affections be more strongly fixed upon her mother in consequence of the discipline of the preceding day? As she is playing about the room, will she be likely to forget the lesson that she has been taught, and again reach out her hand to a forbidden object? Such an act of discipline tends to establish a general principle in the mind of the child, which will be of permanent operation, extending its influence to every command, and promoting the general authority of the mother and the subjection of the child.

I know that some mothers say that they have not time to pay so much attention to their children. But the fact is that not one third of the time is required to take care of an orderly family, which is necessary to take care of a disorderly one. To be faithful in the government of your family is the only way to save time. Can you afford to be distracted and harassed by continued disobedience? Can you spare the time to have your attention called away, every moment, from the business in which you are engaged, by the mischievousness of your willful children?

Look at the parent surrounded by a family of children who are in the habit of doing as they please. She is very busily employed, I will suppose, upon some article of dress, which it is important should be immediately finished. Every moment she is compelled to raise her eyes from her work, to see what the children are doing. Samuel is climbing upon the table. Jane is drawing out the andirons. John is galloping about the room upon the tongs. The mother, almost deafened with noise, wonders what makes her children so much more troublesome than those of other people.

"Jane, let those andirons alone," she exclaims. Jane runs away for a moment, chases Charles around the room, and returns to her mischief. "Charles, put back those tongs." Charles pays no heed to the direction.

The mother, soon seeing how he is wearing the carpet and bruising the furniture, gets up, gives Charles a shake, and places the tongs in their proper situation; but by the time she is fairly seated, and at her work again, Charles is astride the shovel, and traveling at the top of his speed.

I need not continue this picture. But everyone knows that it is not exaggerated. Such scenes often occur. Thousands of immortal spirits are trained up in this turbulence, and anarchy, and noise, for time and for eternity. Now this mother will say to you that she has not time to bring her children into subjection. Whereas, had she been faithful with each individual child, and thus early trained them all to the habit of obedience, she would have saved herself an immense amount of time and toil;— time and toil now vainly expended in attempts to re-establish her authority.

The truth is that though maintaining a proper discipline in a family requires time, and in some cases perhaps may require time which cannot be very conveniently spared, yet on the whole, it is the best possible course for the mother to pursue to save time. A mother whose family is in the condition above described can have no time really at her command.

We will suppose the case of another mother, who has the same work to perform. She has taught her children prompt and implicit obedience. She gives three of them perhaps some blocks, in one corner of the room, and tells them that they may play "build houses," but, that they must not make much noise, and must not interrupt her, for she wishes to be busy.

The other three she places in another corner of the room, with their slates, saying to them that they may play "make pictures." The children, accustomed to such orderly arrangements, employ themselves very quietly and happily for perhaps three quarters of an hour. The mother goes on uninterrupted in her work. Occasionally she raises her eyes and says an encouraging word to her children, now noticing the little architects in the corner, and now glancing her eye at the drawings upon the slates; thus showing the children that she sympathizes with them, and takes an interest in their enjoyments. The children are pleased and happy. The mother is undisturbed.

She does not allow them to continue their amusements till they are weary of them. But after they have played perhaps three quarters of an hour, she says, "Come, children, you have played long enough; you may take up your little blocks and put them away in the drawer." "O, mother," says Maria, "let me play a little while longer, for I have got my house almost done."

"Very well, you may finish it," says the mother, "but tell me as soon as it is done."

In a few minutes Maria says, " There, mamma, see what a large house I have built." The mother looks at the edifice, and adds a pleasant word of encouragement, and then directs the builders to put all their blocks away in their proper place.

She requests the children with the slates to hang them up, and to put away their pencils; so that, the next day, when slates and blocks are wanted, no time may be lost in searching for them.

Now which mother has the most time? and which mother has the happiest time? And which mother will find the most comfort in the subsequent character and affection of her children?

Perhaps someone will say, this is a pleasing picture, but where are we to look for the reality? It is indeed to be regretted that such scenes are of so infrequent occurrence. But it is far from being true that they do not occur. There are many such families of happy parents and affectionate children. And these families are not confined to the wealthy and the learned. It requires not wealth, and it requires not extensive learning, to train up such a family. The principle of government is simple and plain.

It is to begin with enforcing obedience to every command. It is to establish the principle that a mother's word is never to be disregarded. Every judicious parent will, indeed, endeavor to gratify her children in their reasonable wishes. She will study to make them happy; but she will never allow them to gratify themselves in contradiction to her wishes.

But she will not fail to seize upon the occasion to instill into their minds a lesson of obedience. To illustrate this, let us refer to the children playing with the blocks. The mother directs them to put up the blocks. Maria asks permission to play a few moments longer, till she can finish her house.

The mother, desirous of making her children as happy as she can, grants this reasonable wish. Here is a judicious indulgence. But suppose again that the children had continued playing without regard to their mother's command. They intend, perhaps, to continue their amusement only till they complete the pile then in progress. Here is an act of direct disobedience. The children are consulting their own inclinations instead of the commands of their mother. A judicious parent will not allow such an act to pass unnoticed or unpunished. She may perhaps think, considering the circumstances of the case, that a reprimand is all that is.

Is it said that by noticing such little things a mother must be continually finding fault? But it is not a little thing for a child to disobey a mother's commands. This one act of disregarding authority prepares the way for another. It is the commencement of evil which must be resisted. The very first appearances of insubordination must be checked. There are doubtless cases of trifling faults occurring, which a wise parent will judge it expedient to overlook. Children will sometimes be thoughtless and inadvertent.

They will occasionally err from strict propriety, without any real intention of doing wrong. Judgment is here requisite in deciding what things must be overlooked; but we may be assured, I think, that direct and open disobedience is not, in any case, to be classed among the number of trifling faults. The eating of an apple banished our first parents from paradise. The atrocity of the offense consisted in disobedience of a divine command.

Now, every mother has power to obtain prompt obedience if she commences with her children when they are young. They are then entirely in her hands. All their enjoyments are at her disposal. God has thus given her all the power that she needs, to govern and guide them. We have endeavored to show, by the preceding illustrations, that the fundamental principle of government is, when you do give a command, invariably insist upon obedience. And God has given every mother the power to enforce this principle. He has placed in your hands a helpless babe, entirely dependent upon you; so that if it disobeys you, all you have to do is to cut off its sources of enjoyment, or to inflict bodily pain, so steadily and so invariably that disobedience and suffering shall be indissolubly connected in the mind of the child. What more power can a parent ask for than that which God has already given him? And if we fail to use this power for the purposes for which it was bestowed, the sin is ours, and upon us and upon our children must rest the consequences. The exercise of discipline must often be painful, but if you shrink from duty here, you expose yourself to all that sad train of woes which disobedient children leave behind them.

If you cannot summon sufficient resolution to deprive them of enjoyment, and inflict pain when it is necessary, then you must feel that a broken heart and an old age of sorrow will not be unmerited. And when you look upon your dissolute sons and ungrateful daughters, you must remember that the time was when you might have checked their evil propensities. If you love momentary ease better than your children's welfare and your own permanent happiness, you cannot murmur at the lot which you will have freely chosen. And when you meet your children at the bar of God, and they point to you and say, "

It was through your neglect of duty that we are banished from heaven, and consigned to endless woe," you must feel what no tongue can tell. Ah! it is dreadful for a mother to trifle with duty. Eternal destinies are committed to your trust. The influence which you are now exerting will continue unchecked by the grave or the judgment, and will extend onward through those ages to which there is no end.

# 3

# Maternal Authority (Continued)

UPON the subject of obedience there are a few other suggestions of importance to be made.

## Diversity in the Natures of Children

First, there is a very great diversity in the natural dispositions of children. Some are very tender in their feelings, and easily governed by Others are naturally independent and self-willed. Sometimes a child gets its passions excited and its will determined, and it cannot be subdued but by a very great effort. Almost every faithful mother is acquainted with such contests, and she knows that they often form a crisis in the character of the child. If the child then obtain the victory, it is almost impossible for the mother afterward to regain her authority.

The child feels that he is the victor, and his mother the vanquished; and it is with very great difficulty that he will be compelled to renounce his independence. If, on the other hand, the mother conquer, and the child is subdued, he feels that the question is settled, and he has but little disposition to resume hostilities with one who has proved herself superior. I have known many such contests, severe and protracted, which were exceedingly painful to a parent's feelings. But, when once entered upon, they must be continued till the child is subdued. It is not safe, on any account, for the parent to give up and retire vanquished.

The following instance of such a contest is one which really occurred. A gentleman, sitting by his fireside one evening, with his family around him, took the spelling-book and called upon one of his little sons to come and read. John was about four years old. He knew all the letters of the alphabet perfectly, but happened at that moment to be in rather a sullen humor, and was not at all disposed to gratify his father. Very reluctantly he came as he was bid, but when his father pointed with his pencil to the first letter of the alphabet, and said, "What letter is that, John?" he could get no answer. John looked upon the book, sulky and silent.

"My son," said the father pleasantly, "you know the letter A." " I cannot say A," said John.

"You must," said the father, in a serious and decided tone. "What letter is that?"

John refused to answer. The contest was now fairly commenced. John was willful, and determined that he would not read. His father knew that it would be ruinous to his son to allow him to conquer. He felt that he must, at all hazards, subdue him. He took him into another room, and punished him. He then returned, and again showed John the letter. But John still refused to name it. The father again retired with his son, and punished him more severely. But it was unavailing; the stubborn child still refused to name the letter, and when told that it was A, declared that he could not say A. Again the father inflicted punishment as severely as he dared to do it, and still the child, with his whole frame in agitation, refused to yield. The father was suffering from the most intense solicitude. He regretted exceedingly that he had been drawn into the contest.

He had already punished his child with a severity which he feared to exceed. And yet the willful sufferer stood before him, sobbing and trembling, but apparently as unyielding as a rock. I have often heard that parent mention the acuteness of his feelings at that moment. His heart was bleeding at the pain which he had been compelled to inflict upon his son. He knew that the question was now to be settled, who should be master. And after his son had withstood so long and so much, he greatly feared the result.

The mother sat by, suffering, of course, most acutely, but perfectly satisfied that it was their duty to subdue the child, and that in such a trying hour a mother's feelings must not interfere. With a heavy heart the father again took the hand of his son to lead him out of the room for farther punishment. But, to his inconceivable joy, the child shrunk from enduring any more suffering, and cried, "Father, I'll tell the letter." The father, with feelings not easily conceived, took the book and pointed to the letter.

"A," said John, distinctly and fully.

"And what is that?" said the father, pointing to the next letter. "J," said John.

"And what is that?" "C," he continued.

"And what is that?" pointing again to the first letter.

"A," said the now humble child.

"Now carry the book to your mother, and tell her what the letter is." "What letter is that, my son," said the mother.

"A," said John. He was evidently perfectly subdued. The rest of the children were sitting by, and they saw the contest, and they saw where was the victory. And John learnt a lesson which he never forgot—that his father had an arm too strong for him. He learned never again to wage such an unequal warfare. He learnt that it was the safest and happiest course for him to obey.

But perhaps someone says it was cruel to punish the child so severely. Cruel! It was mercy and love. It would indeed have been cruel had the father, in that hour, been unfaithful, and shrunk from his painful duty. The passions which he was then, with so much selfsacrifice, striving to subdue, if left unchecked, would, in all probability, have been a curse to their possessor, and have made him a curse to his friends.

It is by no means improbable that upon the decisions of that hour depended the character and happiness of that child for life, and even for eternity. It is far from improbable that, had he then conquered, all future efforts to subdue him would have been in vain, and that he would have broken away from all restraint, and have been miserable in life, and lost in death. Cruelty! The Lord preserve children from the tender mercies of those who so regard such self-denying kindness. It is always best, however, if possible, to avoid such collisions.

Many children are taught implicit obedience, without ever entering into such a contest with their parents. And it is certainly preferable to govern a child by the mild procedure of ordinary discipline, rather than enter into such a formidable conflict, where great severity is often required. Wisdom, therefore, teaches us to guard against giving a child an opportunity of summoning all its energies to disobey. They are peculiar occasions, and peculiar moods of mind, which generally elicit this strength of rebellious feeling.

A little foresight will often enable us, without surrender of authority, to calm the rising feeling, instead of exciting it to its utmost strength. We may sometimes, by judicious management, check the rebellion in its first appearance, before it has gained sufficient strength to call all power into exercise to put it down. As an illustration, let us suppose that James and Mary are playing together in the evening, and James gets vexed and strikes his sister. He has done this without any provocation, and ought to be punished, and to ask his sister's forgiveness. But the mother has perceived that, during the whole day, James has manifested a very un-amiable disposition.

He has been irritable and unyielding. She sees that now he is excited and angry. Every parent knows that such variations of feeling are not uncommon. One day a child is gentle and affectionate; the next everything seems to go wrong; little things vex and irritate him, and his whole disposition seems to be soured. The mother now, in the case in question, perceives that her son is in this frame of mind. He has done wrong, and he ought to ask his sister's forgiveness; but she knows that, in this excited and un-amiable frame of mind, he will be strongly tempted to resist her authority if she requires him to do so. Unreasonably vexed as he is, it would be one of the hardest acts of submission for him to ask the forgiveness of his sister.

If the mother requires him to do so, the temptation is so strong, that, in all probability, he will refuse to obey. She must then punish him. And here comes the contest, which must be continued, if it is commenced, till the child submits. Now, how is this contest to be avoided? By overlooking the fault? Most certainly not. The mother rises, takes James by the hand, and says, "My son, you have been doing very wrong; you are ill-humored, and must not stay with us any longer: I will carry you to bed." She accordingly leads him away to his chamber.

Just before leaving him for the night, she says to him in a kind but sorrowful tone, how much she is displeased, and how much God must be displeased with his conduct. As usual, she hears him say his prayers, or kneels by the bedside and prays herself that God will forgive him. She then leaves him to his own reflections and to sleep. He is thus punished for his fault. And as he lies in his bed, and hears his brothers and sisters playing happily together below stairs, he feels how much wiser and better it is to be a good boy. In the morning he awakes. Night has given repose to his excited feelings. He thinks how unhappy his yesterday's misconduct made him, and resolves to be more upon his guard for the future. All his rebellious feelings are quelled by the soothing influence of sleep. His passions are not aroused. The mother can now operate upon his mind without any fear of having a contest with a determined and stubborn will.

When the children come down in the morning, she calls James and Mary before her. Taking the hand of each, she mildly says, "My son, you made us all unhappy last night by striking your sister; I hope you are sorry for what you did."

"Yes, mother, I am," says James; being led easily now to the feelings of penitence and submission, to which, during the moments of irritation and excitement, he could not, at least without great difficulty, have been driven. Thus, by judicious management, the desired object is attained, and perfectly attained, while the contest is avoided. The fault is not overlooked, and James is humbled. But had the mother, regardless of the child's peculiar state of feeling, commanded him immediately to ask forgiveness of his sister, it would, in all probability, have led to a scene acutely painful to both mother and son. And the final effect of the discipline would, perhaps, have been less beneficial upon the mind of the child than the course which was actually pursued. But cases will sometimes occur when it is not possible thus to wave the strife.

When such an emergency rises, it is the duty of the parent boldly and resolutely to meet it. If, from false feeling, you shrink from this duty, you are recreant to the sacred trust which God has committed to your care. Is it kindness for a mother to let her child die, rather than compel it to take the bitter prescription which is to restore it to health and strength? And is it kindness to let those passions conquer, which, unsubdued, will be, for time and eternity, a scourge to their possessor? If there be any cruelty in the world which is truly frightful, it is the cruelty of a falsely indulgent and unfaithful parent.

Let it be particularly understood, however, in respect to the subject of formal and settled contests between parents and children, that though firmness and decision are absolutely necessary on the part of parents, when such contests unavoidably arise, they can and they ought to be in most cases avoided. If, for instance, a child disobeys you, you can simply punish it for the act of disobedience, and there let the difficulty end. It is not necessary that you should always require that the thing at first commanded should be done.

You direct a little girl to give a book to her sister. She refuses; and you may take two distinct courses to maintain your violated authority. You may go and take the book yourself and give it to the sister, and then inflict such a punishment upon the disobedient one as the offense deserves. Or, you may insist upon obedience; and to enforce it, enter upon a contest which may be long and painful. Now, whichever of these plans you adopt, be firm and decided in the execution of it. The former is, however, in almost all cases, the wisest and best.

In the above remarks, allusion has been made to the variations of feeling to which children are subject. No one, who has had anything to do with education, can have failed to observe this. In fact, these fluctuations of feeling are by no means peculiar to the earlier stages of life. Almost everyone is conscious of seasons when he seems to be afflicted with a kind of morbid sensitiveness. Our spirits often rise and fall with the state of the bodily health; and he has gained a great victory over his body, and a great triumph of mind, who can invariably preserve the same calm and cheerful spirit, undisturbed by harassing cares, or by the irritations of a diseased frame.

The nervous system of some individuals is so delicately constructed, that an east wind, or a damp day, will completely unhinge the mind. When we see that some of the wisest and best of men are oppressed with these infirmities, we must learn forbearance and sympathy with children. At such times, a judicious mother, knowing that the irritability is as much a bodily as a mental infirmity, will do all in her power to calm and soothe the ruffled spirit. She will avoid everything calculated to irritate the feelings, and will endeavor, by gentle amusements, or by the influence of repose, to lull these feelings to sleep. By this method she will save the child much unhappiness, and will greatly promote the cultivation of an amiable and sweet disposition. The heart of a child is of too delicate a texture to be handled with a rough and careless grasp. Its affectionate and gentle feelings should be elicited by maternal sympathy and love. And we should endeavor to assuage its occasional irritability, by calling away the mind from objects of unpleasant excitement, and alluring it to cheering contemplations.

It is clear that there is a striking difference in the natural dispositions of children; but nothing can be more evident than that a good disposition may be permanently changed by harsh and vexatious measures, while on the other hand, a child of naturally un-amiable feelings may, by judicious culture, become mild and lovely. The cultivation of the disposition is an important part of education. Hence the necessity of studying the moods and the feelings of the child, and of varying the discipline to meet these changes. Cases will undoubtedly arise, when the parent will find it difficult to judge what is duty. Such cases will, however, be infrequent.

The obvious general policy is, when a child is in this excited state, to remove him as much as possible from the power of temptation. And if he commits a fault which it is necessary to notice, let the punishment be of such a kind as is calculated to soothe and quiet him. For instance, give him a comfortable seat by the fire, and require him not to leave the chair for half an hour. Place in his hand some pleasing book, or give him some plaything which will amuse him. By this means you will show that though you find it necessary to subject him to confinement, you cherish no vindictive or resentful feelings against him, and so you awaken no resentment in his heart. In this way the punishment is adapted to the peculiarity of the moral disorder.

Nor would such a confinement as this be a mere mockery of punishment, as it might at first seem. The child feels it to be a real punishment, while still he is not irritated by it. In some cases even, faults may be committed, in circumstances such as we have supposed, which it would be best not to notice at all. A boy may speak peevishly to his sister. The mother does not appear to notice it; she, however, sees the importance of immediately allaying this peevish spirit, and she endeavors to plan some amusement which will promote good humor. Perhaps she lays down her work and joins the children in their amusements, till, through her happy influence, cheerfulness and good-humor are restored.

"Here, my son," she says, " I should like to have you take your slate, and sit down in your chair, and see if you can draw some animal so correctly that I can tell what it is. And Maria, you may take your slate and chair, and sit by his side, and do the same."

The children are quite animated with their new play. They are soon busily at work, and whispering together, that their mother may not hear their conversation and learn by it what animals they are drawing. By this simple artifice the little cloud of irritated feeling which was rising, is entirely dispelled. Had the mother, on the other hand, punished the child for the incidental peevishness of remark, his mind would not have been so speedily or so pleasantly brought into its desired state. Or, had the mother taken no notice of the occurrence, the disposition of the child would have been injured by the continuance and perhaps increase of the ill-humor. Very probably an open quarrel might soon have ensued. Constant watchfulness, on the part of the mother, will enable her thus to foresee many dangers, and prevent many difficulties.

## Never Punish for Accidental Wrongs

Never punish a child when it has not intentionally done wrong. Children are often very unjustly punished. Things which are really wrong are sometimes overlooked, and at others punishment is inflicted on account of some accident, when the child is entirely innocent of any intentional wrong. Such a course of procedure not only destroys, in the mind of the child, the distinction between accident and crime, but is in itself absolutely iniquitous. The parent possesses all power, and she may act as a relentless tyrant, while the child can have no redress.

There is no oppression more cruel than that often thus exercised by passionate parents over their children.

It is very frequently the case that a mother, who does not intend to be guilty of injustice, neglects to make a proper distinction between faults and accidents. A child is playing about the room, and accidentally tears its clothes, or breaks a window with the ball which it is allowed to play with upon the floor. The mother, vexed with the trouble which the accident will cause her, hastily punishes the child. A child may indeed be careless, and so criminally careless as to deserve punishment. But in that case, the punishment ought to be inflicted in such a manner as to show very clearly that it was the carelessness and not the accident that incurred it. To punish an accident is a great injustice;—it is an injustice, however, that is far more extensively practiced than is generally imagined. In fact, perhaps the most common cause of unjust punishment, is confounding the accidental consequences of an act with the real guilt which a child incurred while performing that act.

Parents are very prone to punish carelessness in their children, when it leads to any evil consequences, and to overlook it when it is harmless in its results. A girl, for instance, is placed in charge of an infant. She leaves it and goes away a moment to play. The mother sees that she has gone, and calls her back, only chiding her for her neglect of duty, because no harm was done. If the infant had fallen down and been hurt, the girl would have been punished.

We are all too much inclined to estimate guilt by consequences. A child, for example, who has been permitted to climb upon the chairs, and take things from the table, accidentally pushes off" some valuable article. The mother punishes him severely. Now, where did this child do wrong? His mother had not taught him that he must not climb up to the table. Of course, in the act of climbing there was no disobedience, and the child could not have been conscious, while doing it, that he was doing anything improper If merely a book had fallen, probably no notice would have been taken of the case. But the simple fact that one article fell instead of another, cannot alter the nature of the offense. If it had been the most valuable watch which had fallen, and thus had been entirely ruined, if it had occurred purely through accident, the child deserves no punishment.

Perhaps someone says, there is no need of arguing a point which is so clear. But is it not clear that such acts of injustice are very frequent? And is not almost every mother conscious that she is not sufficiently guarded upon this point? A mother must have great control over her own feelings—a calmness and composure of spirit not easily disturbed—or she will be occasionally provoked to acts of injustice by the misfortunes of which her children are the innocent cause.

Does anyone ask what should be done in such cases as the one referred to? The answer is plain. Children ought to be taught not to do what will expose property to injury; and then, if they do what is thus prohibited, consider them guilty, whether injury results or not.

If the child, in the above-named case, had been so taught, this would have been an act of direct disobedience. And a faithful mother would probably pursue some such course as this. Without any manifestation of anger, she would calmly and seriously say to her son, "My son, I have often told you that you must not climb upon the table. You have disobeyed me."

"But, mother," says the son, "I did not mean to do any harm." "I presume you did not, rny son; I do not accuse you of doing harm, but of having disobeyed me. The injury was accidental, and you are not accountable for it; but the disobedience was deliberate, and very wrong. I am very sorry to punish you, but I must do it. It is my duty." She would then punish him, either by the infliction of pain, or by depriving him, for a time, of some of his usual privileges or enjoyments. The punishment, however, would be inflicted for the disobedience, and not for the accident which attended the disobedience. The child could not but feel that he was justly condemned.

But the question still remains, what is to be done, upon the original supposition that the child had never been taught that it was wrong to climb upon the table, or to throw his ball about the room? In that case the mother has, manifestly, no right even to censure the child. The fault is hers, in not having previously taught him the impropriety of such conduct. All that she can now do, is to improve the opportunity which the occasion presents, to show him the danger of such amusements, and forbid them in future.

If the child be very young, the mother will find it necessary occasionally to allude to the accident and to the rule which she had been led to establish by the occurrence of it, that the lesson may be impressed upon the mind of the child. If she were not to do this, the occurrence might soon pass from his memory, and in a few days he might again, through entire forgetfulness, be engaged in his forbidden sports.

Allowance must also be made for the ignorance of a child. You have, perhaps, a little daughter, eighteen months old, who often amuses herself in tearing to pieces some old newspaper which you give her. It is, to her, quite an interesting experiment. Some day you happen to have your attention particularly occupied for a length of time, and at last, on raising your eyes to see what keeps her so quiet upon the floor, you find that she has a very valuable book in her hand, which she has almost entirely ruined; and your first impulse is to punish her, or, at least, severely to reprove her for the injury. But has she really been doing anything deserving of punishment or censure? Certainly not.

How can she know that it is proper for her to tear one piece of paper, but wrong for her to tear another? She has been as innocently employed as she ever was in her life. The only proper thing to be done, in such a case, is to endeavor to teach the child that a book must be handled with care, and must not be torn. But how can she be taught this without punishing her? She may be taught by the serious tone of your voice, and the sad expression of your countenance, that she has been doing something which you regret. In this way she may be easily taught the difference between a book and a newspaper.

A little boy, about two years of age, was in the habit of amusing himself by scribbling upon paper with a pencil. The father came into the room one day, and found that the little fellow had exceedingly defaced a new book. The marks of his pencil were all over it. Perfectly unconscious of the mischief which he was doing, the child continued his employment as the father entered. In many cases, the parent, in irritation, would have roughly taken the book away, and inflicted a severe blow upon the cheek of the child. I thought I perceived that this was the first emotion in the mind of this parent, though he was of an unusually calm and collected spirit. If it was, however, he immediately saw its impropriety; for, approaching his child, he said, in a perfectly mild and pleasant tone, "O! my son! my son! you are spoiling the book."

The child looked up in amazement.

"That is a book, my son; you must not write upon that. See here," turning over the leaves, "you will spoil father's book. Here is some paper for you. You may write upon this, but you must never write in the book."

The father then took the book, injured as it was, and laid it aside, without any exhibition of excited feeling. Now, how manifestly is this the proper course to pursue, in such a case; and yet how few children are there who, in such circumstances, would have escaped undeserved punishment.

These illustrations are sufficient to show the importance of making allowance for ignorance, and for accidents. And they also show how frequently children suffer, when they are not to blame. If a child is punished when innocent, as well as when guilty, the distinction between right and wrong is obliterated from his mind. Hence it becomes an important rule in family government, never to punish the child unless he has intentionally and knowingly done wrong.

## Never Think That Your Child is Too Young to Understand

We are ingenious in framing excuses for neglecting our duty with our children. At one time they are too young; again they are too sick. Some parents always find an excuse, of one kind or another, for allowing their children to have their own way. A child may, at a very early age, be taught obedience. We can easily teach even a kitten, or a little dog, that it must not touch the meat which is placed before the fire, that it must leave the room when bidden, and a thousand other acts of ready obedience. A Frenchman, it is said, has recently collected a large number of canary birds for a show. He has taught them such implicit obedience to his voice, as to march them in platoons across the room, and directs them to the ready performance of many simple maneuvers.

Now, can it be admitted that a child, fifteen months or two years of age, is inferior in understanding to a canary bird! And must the excuse be made for such a child, that he does not know enough to be taught obedience? A very judicious mother, who has brought up a large family of children, all of whom are now in situations of respectability and usefulness, remarked that it was her practice to obey her children for the first year of their life, but ever after that she expected them to obey her.

She, of course, did not mean by this remark, that the moment the child was one year of age, a sudden and total change took place in her management. During the early months of its infancy she considered it to be her duty to do everything in her power to make the child comfortable and happy. She would endeavor to anticipate all its wants. She would be obedient to the wishes of the child. But, by the time the child was one year of age, she considered it old enough to be brought under the salutary regulations of a well-disciplined family.

I am aware that many parents will say that this is altogether too early a period to commence the government of a child, and others equally numerous, perhaps, will say that it is too late; that a beginning should be made at a much earlier period. In fact, the principle which really ought to guide in such a case, is this: that the authority of the mother ought to be established over the child as soon as it is able to understand a command or prohibition expressed by looks and gestures.

This is at a much earlier period than most parents imagine. Let the mother who doubts it try the experiment, and see how easily she can teach her child that he must not touch the tongs or andirons; or that, when sitting in her lap at table, he must not touch the cups and saucers. A child may be taught obedience in such things then, as well as at any period of its life. And how much trouble does a mother save herself, by having her child thus early taught to obey! How much pain and sorrow does she save her child by accustoming it, in its most tender years, to habits of prompt obedience.

## Guard Against Too Much Punishment

Guard against too much By pursuing a steady course of efficient government, severity will very seldom be found necessary.

If, when punishment is necessary, it is inflicted with composure and with solemnity, occasions for punishment will be very infrequent. Let a mother ever be affectionate and mild with her children. Let her sympathize with them in their little sports. Let her gain their confidence by her assiduous efforts to make them happy. And let her feel, when they have done wrong, not irritated, but sad; and punish them in sorrow, but not in anger. Fear is a useful and necessary principle in family government. God makes use of it in governing his creatures. But it is ruinous to the disposition of a child, exclusively to control him by this motive.

How unhappy must be that family where the parent always sits with a face deformed with scowls, and where the voice is always uttered in tones of severity and command! Such parents we often see. Their children fear them. They are always under restraint in their presence; and home becomes to them an irksome prison, instead of the happy retreat of peace and joy. But where the mother greets her children with smiles; and rewards their efforts to please her, with caresses; and addresses them in tones of mildness and affection, she is touching those chords in the human heart which vibrate in sweet harmony; she is calling into action the noblest and the loveliest principles of our nature. And thus does she prepare the way for every painful act of discipline to come with effectual power upon the heart.

The children know that it gives her pain to punish .them. In all cases in which it can be done, children should 'thus be governed by kindness. But when kindness fails, and disobedience ensues, let not the mother hesitate for a moment to fall back upon her last resort, and punish as severely as is necessary. A few such cases will teach almost any child how much better it is to be obedient than disobedient.

By being thus consistent and decided in government, and commencing with the infancy of each child, in all ordinary cases great severity may be avoided. And it is never proper for a parent to be harsh, and unfeeling, and forbidding, in her intercourse with her children. The most efficient family government may be almost entirely administered by affection, if it be distinctly understood that disobedience cannot pass unpunished. I cannot but pity those unhappy children who dare not come to their parents in confidence and love; who are continually fearing stern looks and harsh words; and who are consequently ever desirous to get away from home, that they may enjoy themselves.

Every effort should be made to make home the most happy place to them; to gather around it associations of delight; and thus to form in the mind of your child an attachment for peaceful and purifying enjoyments. This will most strongly fortify his mind against vice.

And when he leaves the paternal roof, he will ever look back with fond recollections to its joys, and with gratitude to those who made it the abode of so much happiness. In future years, too, when your children become the heads of families, they will transmit to their children the principles which you have implanted. Thus may the influence of your instructions extend to thousands yet unborn.

How little do we think of the tremendous responsibilities which are resting upon us; and of the wide influence, either for good or for evil, which we are exerting! We are setting in operation a train of causes which will go down through all coming time. Long after we have gone to our eternal home, our words and our actions will be aiding in the formation of character. We cannot then arrest the causes which our lives have set in progress, and they will go on elevating immortals to virtue and to heaven, or urging them onward in passion, and sin, and woe.

# 4

# The Mother's Difficulties

THE remarks which have already been made are so obvious, that one is led to inquire, Why is family government generally so defective? Why do so few succeed in obtaining prompt obedience from their children? There are many causes operating to produce this result. The rules of discipline may be simple and plain, and yet many motives may influence us to shrink from enforcing them.

## Lack of Self-control

One great obstacle is the want of self-control on the part of How few persons are there who have gained that conquest over self, which enables them to meet the various vicissitudes of life with calmness and composure! How few are there who are not, occasionally at least, thrown off their guard, and provoked to the exhibition of excited and irritated feeling! And can a mother expect to govern her child when she cannot govern herself? Family government must most emphatically begin at home. It must begin in the bosom of the parent. She must learn to control herself; to subdue her own passions; she must set her children an example of meekness and of equanimity, or she must reasonably expect that all her efforts to control their passions will be ineffectual.

A child gets irritated and strikes his sister; and the mother gets irritated and whips the child. Now, both mother and child have been guilty of precisely the same sin. They have both been angry, and both in anger have struck another. And what is the effect of this sinful punishment? It may make the child afraid to strike his sister again; but will it teach that child that he has done wrong; that it is wicked to be angry? Can it have any salutary effect upon his heart? He sees that his mother is irritated, and thus is he taught that it is proper for him to be angry. He sees that when his mother is irritated she strikes; and thus is he taught that the same course is proper for him.

The direct effect of the punishment is to feed the flame and strengthen the inveteracy of passion. In such a course as this there is no moral instruction, and no salutary discipline. And yet a mother who has not conquered self, who cannot restrain the violence of her own passions, will often inflict punishments like these. When we see such a mother with passionate and turbulent children, no second question need be asked why they are not gentle and obedient. And when we reflect how very few there are who may not be occasionally provoked to act from the irritation of the moment, we cannot wonder that the family so often presents a scene of uproar and misrule. This habit of self-control, at all times, and under all circumstances, is one of the most important and most difficult things to be acquired.

Many parents have, from infancy, been unaccustomed to restraint, and they find a very great struggle to be necessary to smother those feelings which will sometimes rise almost involuntarily. But we should ever remember that this must be done, or we cannot be faithful to our children. We must bring our own feelings and our own actions under a system of rigid discipline, or it will be in vain for us to hope to curb the passions and restrain the conduct of those who are looking to us for instruction and example. There will many cases occur which will exceedingly try a mother's patience. Unless naturally blest with a peculiarly quiet spirit, or habituated from early life to habits of self-government, she will find that she has very much to do with her own heart.

This point we would most earnestly urge, for it is of fundamental importance. Anger is temporary insanity. And what can be more deplorable than to see a mother in the paroxysm of irritation, taking vengeance on her child? Let a mother feel grieved, and manifest her grief when her child does wrong. Let her, with calmness and reflection, use the discipline which the case requires. But never let her manifest irritated feeling, or give utterance to an angry expression. If her own mind is thus kept serene and unimpassioned, she will instruct by example as well as precept. She will easily know, and more judiciously perform her duty. And the superiority of her own conduct will command the respect and the admiration of her children. Until this is done, it will be impossible for a mother to enforce the rules of discipline, simple and obvious as those rules are.

## Lack of Resolution

Another great obstacle in the way is the want of resolution. It is always painful to a parent's feelings to deprive a child of any reasonable enjoyment, or to inflict pain. Hence we are ingenious in framing apologies to relieve ourselves from this Your child does wrong, and you know that he ought to be punished; but you shrink from the duty of inflicting the punishment. Now, of what avail is it to be acquainted with the rules of discipline, if we cannot summon resolution to enforce those rules? It will do no good to read one book and another upon the subject of education, unless we are willing, with calm and steady decision, to punish our children when the occasion requires. It is this weak indulgence, this wicked refusal to perform painful duty, which has ruined thousands of families.

In fact, cases sometimes occur, in which a mother, not content with neglecting herself, to perform her duty to her children, will interpose to prevent her husband from doing it. She will openly remonstrate with the father for punishing a stubborn child. She will call him cruel and unfeeling, and confirm her child in his willfulness, by her wicked sympathy and her caresses.

What can be expected from such a course as this? Such a mother is the most cruel and merciless enemy which her child can have. Under such an influence he will probably grow up in wretchedness, not only to curse the day in which he was born, but to heap still bitterer curses upon the mother who bore him. You can do nothing more ruinous to your child; you can do nothing which will more effectually teach him to hate and despise you; you can do nothing which will, with more certainty, bring you in sorrow and disgrace to the grave, than thus to allow maternal feelings to influence you to neglect painful but necessary acts of discipline.

I would ask the mother who reads this book, if she has not often been conscious of a struggle between the sense of duty and inclination. Duty has urged you to punish your child. Inclination has urged you to overlook its disobedience. Inclination has triumphed; and your child has retired victorious, and of course confirmed in his sin. Be assured that thus, in your own heart, lies one of the greatest obstacles to your success; and until this obstacle be surmounted, everything else will be unavailing. It would by no means be difficult to fill this volume with cases illustrative of this fact, and of the awful consequences resulting. A few years since, a lady was left a widow, with several little sons. She loved them most devotedly.

The affliction which she had experienced in the loss of her husband, fixed her affections with more intensity of ardor and sensitiveness upon her children. They were her only hope. Sad and joyless as she was, she could not endure to punish them, or to deprive them of a single indulgence. Unhappy and misguided woman! Could she expect to escape the consequences of such a course? She was living upon the delusive hope that her indulgences would insure their love. And now one of these sons is seventeen years of age, a strong, and turbulent, and self-willed boy. He is altogether beyond the influence of maternal restraint.

He is the tyrant of the family, and his afflicted mother is almost entirely brokenhearted by this accumulation of sorrow. The rest of the children are advancing in the same path. She sees and trembles in view of the calamity, which it is now too late to avert. It would be far happier for her to be childless, as well as a widow. Her children are her oppressors. She is their slave. It is impossible for her now to retrace her steps, or to retrieve the injury which she has done to her children and to herself. Hardly any situation can be conceived more truly pitiable. And what has caused this magnitude of sorrow? Simply the mother's reluctance to do her duty.

She looked upon her poor fatherless children with all the tender emotions of a widowed mother, and could not bear to throw around them necessary restraint, and insist upon obedience to her commands. She knew perfectly well, that when they were disobedient, they ought to be punished; that it was her duty to enforce her authority. It was not her ignorance which caused this dreadful wreck of happiness; it was the want of resolution—that fond, and foolish, and cruel tenderness, which induced her to consult her own feelings, rather that the permanent welfare of her children.

The reader will, perhaps, inquire whether this statement is a true account of a real case. It is a true account of a thousand cases all over our land. Mothers, we appeal to your observation, if you do not see, everywhere around you, these wrecks of earthly hopes. Have we not warnings enough to avoid this fatal rock? and yet it is the testimony of all who have moved about the world with an observing eye, that this parental irresolution is one of the most prominent causes of domestic misery.

Parental discipline should be enforced too, with calmness, energy, and decision, or it will often become inefficient and merely vexatious, so as to do more harm than good. The spirit of the child will be irritated, but not subdued by it. Punishment in such cases becomes a petty vexation, and its influence is most decidedly pernicious. It is of the utmost importance, that when it is inflicted, it should be serious and effectual. And it is certain that the mother who adopts prompt and decisive measures, will go forward with far less trouble to herself and her child, and will, on the whole, inflict far less pain than the one who adopts the feeble and dilatory measures which we see so often resorted to. While the one must be continually threatening, and inflicting that mockery of punishment which is just enough to irritate the temper and spoil the disposition; the other will usually find her word promptly obeyed, and will very seldom find it necessary to punish at all.

Many parents govern, or attempt to govern, by threats. They never punish for the present offence, but are always threatening something terrible for the next one. When the next time comes, there is still no punishment but only new threats for future occasions. Now a government of threats is the worst possible government. Such a system keeps up a continual feeling of irritation and anger between the parent and child, and yet fails wholly to accomplish the ends of efficient discipline.

But few persons have ever exemplified a more correct knowledge of human nature than Napoleon, and but few have ever acquired such a control over the mind. There was once a formidable mob rioting in the streets of Paris, and carrying devastation wherever they went. An officer was sent out with a body of infantry to disperse the mob. He ordered them to retire. They answered him with derision. He threatened to fire upon them. They defied him.

He opened upon them a fire with blank cartridges. As volley after volley was discharged, and not a man fell, the mob laughed to scorn such impotent efforts. At last the general was compelled to load with ball. But by this time the passions of the mob were so excited, and they had become so familiar with the harmless discharge of musketry, that they stood firm when the balls came. They had been gradually prepared for them. A formidable battle was the result; and it was not till after an immense massacre that the infuriated populace was dispersed.

At another time, when the ravages of a Parisian mob were scattering terror through the city, Napoleon himself went to suppress it. He led on, at a quick step, several companies of artillery. Immediately upon arriving at the scene of devastation, the soldiers, retiring to the right and left, opened upon the riotous multitude the formidable cannon. Not a word was said; not a moment of hesitation intervened; but at once the voice of Napoleon was heard in the thunder of the artillery, and the compact mass of the multitude was plowed through by a cannon-ball.

The mob, unprepared for such decisive measures, and terrified at the havoc, fled with the utmost precipitancy in every direction. Then did he pour in his blank cartridges. Peal after peal thundered through the streets, adding to the consternation of the affrighted multitude, and in a very few minutes scarcely a solitary straggler was to be seen. The whole effect was produced by one ball fired at the proper time.

Such was the general character of the measures which this extraordinary man adopted, and which gave him an ascendency over the public mind almost unparalleled in the history of man. Someone afterward suggested to him in respect to the case above described, that it would have been more merciful if he had first tried the effect of blank charges, and then, if necessary, had proceeded to extremities. But he very justly replied that by such tardy measures the mob would have had time to collect their courage, and many more would have fallen before they could have been compelled to fly.

Now the principle illustrated in this anecdote is of universal application. Real benevolence prompts to decisive measures. The mother who first coaxes, then threatens, then pretends to punish, then punishes a little, and finally a little more—is only making trouble for herself and sorrow for her family. But, on the other hand, if she promptly meets acts of disobedience with firmness, and inflicts necessary punishment decidedly, and at once, she is, in the most effectual way, promoting her own happiness, and the best welfare of her child.

A parent is much more prone to be thus fatally indulgent, if a child is of a feeble and sickly constitution. Such children are very frequently spoiled. How strange, when God, in his mysterious providence, lays his hand upon some little one, and causes it to languish in weakness and in suffering, that the parent on that very account should neglect that child's welfare, and allow its passions to grow unchecked, its will to be stubborn and unsubdued! The mother perhaps is willing to do her duty with her more robust son. She will do all in her power to control his passions, and make him a good and happy boy. But the poor little sufferer she will indulge in all its caprices, till passion is strong and irritability is unconquerable, and the deeper sorrows of the mind are thus added to the pains and weakness of the body.

O how much cruelty there is in the world which goes by the false name of tenderness or love. Mother, have you a sick and suffering child? You are to that child a guardian angel, if with mild and affectionate decision you enforce your authority. Punish that child if it be necessary to teach him habitually and promptly to obey. If you do not do this, you are the most dangerous enemy that your child can have. You are doing that which has the most direct tendency to perpetuate its feebleness and to promote its misery. And yet I know that some mothers will still say, "What, speak sternly to, and even punish a poor little child when sick! How unfeeling!"

There, there is the difficulty. Is it unkind for you to do all in your power to make your child patient and happy! A little girl, we will suppose, by some accident is cut deeply in the hand. Her mother is so kind that she will not allow a physician to be called, for fear lest he should hurt her daughter in probing and dressing the wound. Day after day this kind mother beholds the increasing and extending inflammation. She strives in her ignorance to assuage the agony of the wound, till, after many days of excruciating suffering, the physician is finally summoned to save her daughter's life by amputating the limb. When the accident first occurred, a few moments of attention, and the enduring of a trifling pain, would have prevented all these dreadful consequences.

But the conduct of that mother is far more cruel, who will allow the mind's inflammation to increase and extend unchecked; who, rather than inflict the momentary pain which is necessary to subdue the stubborn will, and allay irritation, will allow the moral disorder to gain such strength asto be incurable. The consequences thus ensuing are far more disastrous than those resulting from any bodily injury. They affect man's immortal nature, and go on through eternity. There is no cruelty so destructive as this.

Yet let it not be supposed that austerity is recommended. This is unnecessary, and is always to be avoided. Let the tones of the voice be affectionate and soothing. Let the mother sympathize with her whole heart in the trials and sufferings of her child. Let her be ingenious in devices for its amusement. But let her not ruin her precious treasure by indulging it in peevishness or disobedience. Your child cannot possibly be happy, unless taught to subdue his passions and to be obedient to your will. We would have kindness, and gentleness, and love, ever diffusing joy through the family circle. But if you would see your children happy, and be happy yourself, you must, when your children are in sickness, as well as when they are in health, summon sufficient resolution to insure propriety of behavior and obedience to your commands.

Be invariably firm then in doing your duty. Never be restrained from any duty in the government of your child, because it is painful to maternal feelings to perform it. It is certainly wisely ordered by Providence that it should be painful to a parent's heart to inflict suffering upon a child. He who can punish without sympathy, without emotions of sorrow, cannot punish with a right spirit. Even our Father in heaven does not willingly afflict his children. But does he on that account withhold his discipline, and allow us to go on in sin unpunished? We must, in earnest prayer, look to him for strength and wisdom, and religiously do our duty.

We must be willing to have our own hearts bleed, if we can thus save our children from the ravages of those passions which, unchecked, will ruin their usefulness and peace. A child, a short time since, was taken sick with the dangerous disorder, the croup. It was a child most ardently beloved, and ordinarily very obedient. But in the state of uneasiness and pain produced by the paroxysms of the disease, he refused to take the medicine which it was needful to administer without delay. The father, finding the boy resolute in his disobedience, immediately punished him, sick and suffering as he was. Under these circumstances, and fearing that his son might soon die, it must have been a most severe trial to the father to be compelled to perform this duty. But the consequence was that the child was taught that sickness was no excuse for disobedience. And while his sickness continued, he promptly took whatever medicine was prescribed, and was patient and submissive. Soon the child was well.

Does anyone say that this was cruel? It was one of the noblest acts of kindness which could have been performed. If the father had shrunk from duty here, it is by no means improbable that the life of the child would have been the forfeit. And this is the way to acquire strength of resolution, by practicing strength of resolution in every case. We must readily and promptly do our duty, be it ever so painful.

## Lack of Harmony Between Parents

Another great obstacle in the way of training up a happy and virtuous family is the occasional want of harmony between parents on the subject of education. Sometimes, when a father is anxious to do his duty, the mother is a weak and foolish woman, who thinks that every punishment, and every deprivation of indulgence, is cruelty to her And when anyone of them is punished, she will, by her caresses, destroy the effect of the discipline, and convey to the mind of the child the impression that his father is cruel and unjust. A man who has formed so unhappy a connection, is indeed in a deplorable condition. And if his wife is incapable of being convinced of the ruinous consequences of such a course, he ought to take upon himself the whole duty of government. But as I am not now writing to fathers, I must turn from this case to another.

It not infrequently happens that a judicious and faithful mother is connected with a husband whose general principles and example are of a deleterious character. In such cases, not only does the whole government of the family devolve upon the mother, but the influence of the father is such as, in a great degree, to counteract all her exertions. This is indeed a trying situation. It is, however, far from being a hopeless one. You must not give up in despair, but let the emergencies of the case rouse you to more constant watchfulness, and more persevering and vigorous effort.

If a wife be judicious and consistent in her exertions, a father, in almost all cases, will soon feel confidence in her management of her family, and will very gladly allow her to bear all the burden of taking care of the children. Such a father is almost necessarily, much of the time, absent from home, and when at home, is not often in a mood to enjoy the society of his family. Let the mother in such a case, teach her children to be quiet and still when their father is present. Let her make every effort to accustom them to habits of industry. And let her do everything in her power to induce them to be respectful, and obedient, and affectionate to their father. This course is indeed the best which can be adopted to reclaim the unhappy parent. The more cheerful you can make home to him, the stronger are the inducements which are presented to draw him away from scenes into which he ought not to enter.

It is true there is no situation more difficult than the one which we are now describing. But, that even these difficulties are not insurmountable, facts have not infrequently proved. Many cases occur, in which the mother triumphantly surmounts them all, and rears up a virtuous and happy family. Her husband is, perhaps, most brutally intemperate; and I need not here depict the scenes through which such a mother is called to pass. She sees, however, that the welfare of the family is dependent upon her, and accordingly nerves her heart, resolutely, to meet her responsibilities. She commences, in the earliest infancy of her children, teaching them implicit obedience.

She binds them to her with those ties from which they never would be able or desirous to break. The most abundant success rewards her efforts. The older her children grow, the more respectful and attentive they become, for the more clearly they see that they are indebted to their mother for salvation from their father's disgrace and woe. Every sorrow of such a mother is alleviated by the sympathy and affection of her sons. She looks around upon them with feelings of maternal gratification, which no language can describe.

They feel the worth and the dignity of her character. Though her situation in life may be humble, and though her mind may not be stored with knowledge, her moral worth, and her judicious government, command their reverence.

In a family of this sort, in a neighboring state, one cold December night, the mother was sitting alone by the fire, between the hours of nine and ten, waiting for the return of her absent husband. Her sons, fatigued with the labors of the day, had all retired to rest. A little before ten, her husband came in from the neighboring store, where he had passed the evening with his degraded associates. He insisted upon calling up the boys at that unseasonable hour, to send into the wood lot for a load of wood. Though there was an ample supply of fuel at the house, he would not listen to reason or remonstrance, but stamped with rage, and swore that the boys should go. The mother, finding it utterly in vain to oppose his wishes, called her sons, and told them that their father insisted upon their going with the team to the wood lot. She spoke to them kindly; told them she was sorry that they must go; but, said she, "Remember that he is your father." Her sons were full grown young men. But at their mother's voice they immediately rose, and, without a murmur, brought out the oxen, and went to the woods.

They had perfect confidence in her judgment and her management. While they were absent, their mother was busy in preparing an inviting supper for them upon their return. The drunken father soon retired. About midnight the sons finished their task, and entering the house, found their mother ready to receive them with cheerfulness and smiles. A bright fire was blazing on the hearth. The room was warm and pleasant. With keen appetites and that cheerfulness of spirits which generally accompanies the performance of duty, those children sat down with their much-loved parent to the repast she had provided, and soon after all were reposing in the quietude and the silence of sleep.

Many a mother has thus been the guardian and the savior of her family. She has brought up her sons to industry, and her daughters to virtue. And in her old age she has reaped a rich reward for all her toil, in the affections and attentions of her grateful children. She has struggled, in tears and discouragement, for many weary years, till at last God has dispelled all the gloom, and filled her heart with joy in witnessing the blessed results of her fidelity. Be not, therefore, desponding. That which has once been done may be done again.

From what has been said in this chapter, it appears that self-control and resolution are the two all-important requisites in family government. With these two qualifications, which a person is inexcusable in not possessing, almost every other obstacle may be surmounted Without these, your toil and solicitude will, in all probability, be in vain. Your faithful exertions, attended with God's ordinary blessing, will open to you daily new sources of enjoyment in the unfolding virtues and expanding faculties of your children.

Your decisive government will, most undoubtedly, be rewarded with the affection and respect of those whom you are training up to usefulness and happiness. And when old age comes, your children will welcome you to their homes, and rejoice to give you a seat by their fireside, and by unremitted attentions will do all in their power to prove how deeply they feel that debt of gratitude which never can be fully repaid. Such joys will obliterate the remembrance of all present toils and sorrows. Let these hopes cheer you to go on rejoicing in the path of duty.

# 5

# Faults and Errors

THERE are many faults in family government, which have been handed down from generation to generation, and have become almost universally diffused. They are so general, and we have been so long accustomed to them, that their glaring impropriety escapes our notice. The increasing interest now felt in the subject of education, by leading parents to read and to think, has taught many to avoid those errors which still very generally prevail.

There are many parents who have not facilities for obtaining books upon this subject, and who have not been led to reflect very deeply upon their responsibilities. Some of these errors are such, that an apology seems almost necessary for cautioning mothers against them, since common sense so plainly condemns them. But let it be remembered, how large a portion of the mothers of our land are, by their situation, deprived of those sources of information and excitements to thought, which God has conferred upon others.

## Talking About Children in Their Presence

Do not talk about children in their presence. We are very apt to think that children do not understand what we say to one another, because they are unable to join in the conversation But a child's comprehension of language is far in advance of his ability to use it. I have been much surprised at the result of experiments upon this subject. A little child creeping upon the floor, and who could not articulate a single word, was requested to carry a piece of paper across the room and put it in a chair.

The child perfectly comprehended the direction, and crept across the room, and did as he was bidden. An experiment or two of this kind will satisfy anyone how far a child's mind is in advance of his power to express his ideas. And yet, when a child is three or four years old, parents will relate in their presence shrewd things which they have said and done; sometimes even their acts of disobedience will be mentioned with a smile. The following conversation once passed between a lady and a mother, whose child, three years of age, was standing by her side.

"How does little Charles do? said the lady.

"O," replied the mother, with a smile, "he is doing pretty well, but he is the greatest rogue you ever saw: I can do nothing with him."

"Why," said the lady, "he does not look like a stubborn child." "No," the mother replied, "he has not a bad disposition, but," she continued, smiling, " he is so fond of mischief that I can never make him mind me. He knows that he must not touch the andirons, but just before you came in he went and put one of his fingers on the brass, and looked me directly in the face. I told him he must take off his hand; and he put another finger on. I tried to look cross at him; but he, instead of stopping, rubbed his whole hand over the brass, and then ran away, laughing as heartily as he could. He did it, I suppose, on purpose to plague me, he is such a rogue."

We insert this rather undignified story that the mothers who may read this chapter may know exactly what we mean by the caution we are urging. Now, to say nothing of that maternal unfaithfulness which would permit such acts of disobedience, how ruinous upon the mind of the child must be the effect of hearing his conduct thus spoken of and applauded! This perverse little fellow was more interested in the narration than either mother or visitor, and the impression produced upon his mind was stronger undoubtedly than upon theirs. The child was taught a lesson of disobedience, not soon to be forgotten.

There are many little artifices which a child will practice, which are decidedly to be discountenanced, but which a parent nevertheless can scarce refrain from smiling at when they occur. These proofs of mental quickness and ingenuity are in some sense gratifying to parental feelings. They give promise of a mind susceptible of a high degree of cultivation, if properly guided and restrained. And there are playful and affectionate feats of childhood which are pleasing on every account. They show good feelings, as well as an active intellect.

Parents will speak to one another of those innumerable little occurrences which are daily gratifying them. But if these things are mentioned in the presence of the child, and applauded, its little heart is puffed up with vanity. How slight a degree of flattery is sometimes sufficient to awaken emotions of the most disgusting self-conceit, even in individuals of mature minds! How few persons are there who can bear praise! Vanity is almost a universal sin. None are so low, and none are so high, as to be freed from its power. And can a child bear, uninjured, that praise which has ruined so many men? Here lies one cause of the self-conceit so often visible in the nursery.

We flatter our children without being conscious that they are so greedily drinking in the flattery. We do not give them credit for the amount of understanding which they actually possess. It is true, almost all children are regarded by their parents as unusually intelligent. This arises from the fact, that we are daily observing the unfoldings of the minds of the little ones who surround our firesides, while we have no opportunity of noticing the mental developments of others. But notwithstanding all this strength of parental partiality, we ordinarily consider children far less intelligent than they in reality are; and a mother will often talk as unguardedly in the presence of her child, who is three or four years of age, as she would in the presence of an infant of so many months.

The necessity of caution upon this subject will be obvious to every parent upon a moment's reflection. Let nothing be said in the hearing of a child that would tend to excite its vanity. Guard against the possibility of his supposing that he does and says remarkable things, and is superior to other children.

But though a parent may restrain her own tongue, it is more difficult to restrain the tongues of others. Many visitors make it a constant habit to flatter the children wherever they go. Regardless of the ruinous effects upon their tender and susceptible minds, they think only of pleasing the parents. Beautiful children are thus peculiarly exposed. How common is it for a child of handsome countenance to have a spoiled temper! This is so frequently the case, that many persons have supposed that "spoiled beauty" are words never to be separated.

I once knew a little boy, of unusually bright and animated countenance. Everyone who entered the house, noticed the child, and spoke of his beauty. One day a gentleman called upon business, and being engaged in conversation, did not pay that attention to the child to which he was accustomed, and which he now began to expect as his due. The vain little fellow made many efforts to attract notice, but not succeeding, he at last placed himself full in front of the gentleman, and asked, "Why don't you see how beautiful I be?" The feeling, it is true, is not often so openly expressed, but nothing is more common than for it to be excited in precisely this way. It is surely a duty to approve children when they do right, and to disapprove when they do wrong. But great caution should be used to preserve a child from hearing anything which will destroy that most lovely trait of character —a humble spirit. It is, on this account, often a misfortune to a child to be unusually handsome or forward. It is so difficult to preserve it from the contaminations of flattery, that what might have been a great benefit becomes a serious injury.

JOHN S. C. ABBOTT

## Making Exhibitions of Your Children's Attainments

Do not make exhibitions of your children's attainments. And here we must refer again to the danger of exciting vanity. There is no passion more universal than vanity, or with greater difficulty subdued. An eminent clergyman was once leaving his pulpit, when one of his parishioners addressed him, highly commending the sermon he had just uttered. "Be careful, my friend," said the clergyman, " I carry a tinder-box in my bosom." And if the bosom of an aged man of piety and of prayer may be thus easily inflamed, must there not be great danger in showing off a child to visitors, who will most certainly flatter its performance?

You have taught your daughter some interesting hymns. She is modest and unassuming, and repeats them with much propriety. A friend calls, and you request the child to repeat her hymns. She does it. Thus far there is, perhaps, no injury done. But as soon as she has finished the recitation, your friend begins to flatter the child. Soon another and another friend calls, and the scene is continually repeated, till your daughter feels proud of her performance. She becomes indeed quite an actress. And the hymn which was intended to lead her youthful heart to God does but fill that heart with pride. Must it not be so? How can a child withstand such strong temptations?

Parents may very properly show their children that they are gratified in witnessing their intellectual attainments. And this presents a motive sufficiently strong to stimulate them to action. But when they are exposed to the indiscriminate and injudicious flattery of any who may chance to call, it is not for a moment to be supposed that they will retain just views of themselves. It must however be allowed, that, with some children the danger is much greater than with others. Some need much encouragement, while others need continual restraint. Who has not noticed the thousand arts which a vain child will practice, simply to attract attention? Who has not seen such a spoiled one take a book and read, occasionally casting a furtive glance from the page to the visitor, to see if the studious habit is observed? And can such a child be safely exhibited to strangers?

It may, perhaps, at times, be an advantage to a modest child to repeat a hymn, or something of that nature, to a judicious friend. If your pastor feels that interest in children which he ought to cherish, he will regard all the little ones of his congregation with parental affection. He ought not to be considered as a stranger in the family. Children may appear before him with confidence and affection, and if he has the spirit of his Master, he will cautiously guard against flattery, and endeavor to improve the occasion by leading the mind to serious thoughts. But the practice of making a show of children, of exhibiting their little attainments to attract applause, is certainly reprehensible; and it is, we fear, not only common, but increasing.

The following remarks upon this subject are from the pen of an individual who combines much shrewdness of observation with extensive experience. "I always felt pain for poor little things set up before company to repeat verses, or bits of plays, at six or eight years old. I have sometimes not known which way to look, when a mother, whom I could not but respect on account of her fondness for her child, has forced the feeble-voiced eighth wonder of the world to stand with its little hand stretched out, spouting the soliloquy of Hamlet, or some such thing. I do not know anything much more distressing to the spectators than exhibitions of this sort. Upon these occasions no one knows what to say, or whither to direct his looks.

If I had to declare, which, on the whole, have been the most disagreeable moments of my life, I verily believe that, after due consideration, I should fix upon those in which parents whom I have respected, have made me endure exhibitions like these; for this is your choice, to be insincere, or to give offense. The plaudits which the child receives in such cases puff it up in its own thoughts, and send it out into the world stuffed with pride and insolence, which must and will be extracted from it by one means or another. Now parents have no right thus to indulge their own feelings at the risk of the happiness of their children."

Scenes similar to those above described will at once occur to the recollection of every reader. And the fact that such are the feelings of many strangers, in general, is of itself amply sufficient to discountenance the practice.

There are two extremes which it is necessary to avoid. The one is that of secluding children altogether from society; the other is, of wearying our friends by their presence and their ceaseless talk. If we consider our children as troubles, to be kept out of the way whenever we wish for social enjoyment; if the entrance of a few friends to pass the evening is the signal for their immediate departure to another room, how can we expect them to improve, or to become acquainted with the proprieties of life? They must listen to the conversation and observe the manners of their superiors, that their minds and their manners may be improved.

Not long since I heard a gentleman speaking of an unusually interesting family that he had just visited. It was known that he was coming to pass the evening. As he entered the room he saw three little children sitting quietly and silently by the fire. The mother was sitting by the table with her sewing. The father was rising to receive him. The children remained for an hour or more, listening with interest to the conversation which passed between their parents and the gentleman. They made not the least interruption, but by their presence and cheerful looks contributed much to the enjoyment of the evening. At eight o'clock the mother said, "Children, it is eight." Without another word, they all rose and left the room. The mother soon followed, and after being absent a few moments, returned.

Now how much enjoyment is there in such a family as this! And how much improvement do the children derive from being accustomed to the society of their superiors! In this way they are taught humility, for they see how much less they know than others. They gain information, and their minds are strengthened by the conversation they hear. Their manners are improved, for children learn more by example than precept. If you would enjoy these pleasures, and confer upon your children these benefits, it is indispensable that they be habitually well governed.

Nothing can be more hopeless than to expect that children will conduct properly when company is present, if at other times they are uncontrolled.

Some parents, feeling the importance that their children should enjoy good society, and at the same time having them under no restraint, deprive themselves and their visitors of all enjoyment, and their children of all benefit. We do not like, even in imagination, to encounter the deafening clamor of such a scene. Some ' are lolling about the stranger's chair; some crying; some shouting. The mother is pulling at the gown of one and scolding at another. The visitor, distracted with the noise, endeavors in vain to engage in conversation. The time, and attention, and patience of the parents are absorbed by their lawless family. The visitor, after enduring the uproar for half an hour, is happy in making his escape. Where can there be pleasure, and where can there be profit in such a scene as this?

There are many advantages in encouraging an inquisitive spirit in a child. It has entered upon a world where everything is new and astonishing. Of course it is hourly meeting with objects upon which it desires information. But sometimes when a child finds that his parents encourage him in asking questions, he begins to think that it is a very pretty thing. He will be incessantly presenting his inquiries. His motive will cease to be a gratification of a reasonable and commendable curiosity, and he will desire merely to display his skill, or to talk for the sake of talking. It is very necessary to restrain children in this respect. Their motives are generally distinctly to be seen. And if the motive which prompts the question be improper, let the child receive marks of disapprobation, and not of approval.

"Mother, what is the coffee-pot for?" said a child of three years, at the breakfast table.

"It is to put the coffee in," said the mother.

"And why do you put the coffee in the coffee-pot?"

"Because it is more convenient to pour it out."

"And what," said the child, hesitating and looking around the table to find some new question. "And what—are the cups for?'

"They are to drink from."

"And why do you drink out of the cups?"

In this manner the child, during the whole time allotted for the breakfast, incessantly asked his questions. The mother as continually answered them. She had adopted the principle, that her child must always be encouraged in asking questions. And by blindly and thoughtlessly following out this principle, she was puffing up his heart with vanity, and making him a most unendurable talker.

The common sense principle, to guide us upon this subject, is obvious. If the motive be good, and the occasion suitable, let the child be encouraged in his inquiries. If otherwise, let him be discouraged. A child is sitting at the breakfast table with his father and mother. The mother lifts the top of the coffee-pot, and the child observes the contents violently boiling. "Mother," says the little boy, "what makes the coffee bubble up so?"

Here the motive is good, and the occasion is proper. And one of the parents explains to the child the chemical process which we call the boiling. The parents have reason to be gratified at the observation of the child, and the explanation communicates to him valuable knowledge. But perhaps a stranger is present, with whom the father is engaged in interesting conversation. Under these circumstances, the child asks the same question. It is, however, now unseasonable. He ought to be silent when company is present. The mother accordingly replies, "My son, you should not interrupt your father. You must be perfectly silent, and listen to what he is saying."

She does not, however, forget the question, but embraces some opportunity of again alluding to it. She gives him an answer, and shows him that it is very impolite to interrupt the conversation of others, or to engross attention when company is present. Much pleasure is destroyed, and much improvement prevented, in permitting the conversation of friends to be interrupted by the loquacity of children.

Some parents, to avoid this inconvenience, immediately send their children from the room when visitors arrive. This is treating children with injustice, and the parents must reap the mortifying consequences in their uncultivated manners and uncultivated minds. Hence, in many gentlemen's families, you find awkward and clownish children. If children are banished from pleasing and intelligent society, they must necessarily grow up rude and ignorant. The course to be pursued, therefore, is plain. They should be often present when friends visit you. But they should be taught to conduct properly —to sit in silence and listen. They should not speak unless spoken to. And above all, they should not be thrust forward upon the attention of visitors, to exhibit their attainments, and receive flattery as profusely as your friends may be pleased to deal it out.

## Do Not Deceive Children

Many are unaware of the evil consequences which result from this common practice. A physician once called to extract a tooth from a child. The little boy seeing the formidable instruments, and anticipating the pain, was exceedingly frightened, and refused to open his mouth. After much fruitless solicitation, the physician said, "Perhaps there is no need of drawing it. Let me rub it a little with my handkerchief, and it may be all that is necessary; it will not hurt you in the least." The boy, trusting his word, opened his mouth.

The physician, concealing his instrument in his handkerchief, seized hold of the tooth and wrenched it out. The parents highly applauded his artifice. But the man cheated the child. He abused his confidence, and he inflicted an injury upon his moral feelings not soon to be effaced. Will the child ever believe again what that physician may say? And when told that it is wicked to say that which is not true, will not the remembrance of the doctor's falsehood be fresh in his mind? And while conscious that his parents approved of the deception, will he not feel it to be right for him to deceive, that he may accomplish his desires?

The practice of deceiving children is attended with the most ruinous consequences. It unavoidably teaches the child to despise his parents. After he has detected them in one falsehood, he will not believe them when they speak the truth. It destroys his tenderness of conscience; and it teaches arts of deception. And what are the advantages? Why, in one particular instance, the point is gained.

Let compulsion be resorted to when necessary, but deception never. If a child cannot place implicit confidence in his parent, most assuredly no confidence can be reposed in the child. Is it possible for a mother to practice arts of deception and falsehood, and at the same time her daughter be forming a character of frankness and of truth? Who can for a moment suppose it? We must be what we wish our children to be. They will form their characters from ours.

A mother was once trying to persuade her little son to take some medicine. The medicine was very unpalatable, and she, to induce him to take it, declared it did not taste bad. He did not believe her. He knew, by sad experience, that her word was not to be trusted. A gentleman and friend who was present, took the spoon, and said, "James, this is medicine, and it tastes very badly. I should not like to take it, but I would take it if it was necessary. You have courage enough to swallow something which does not taste good, have you not?"

"Yes," said James, looking a little less sulky. "But that is very bad indeed."

"I know it," said the gentleman, "I presume you never tasted anything much worse." The gentleman then tasted the medicine himself, and said, "It is really very unpleasant. But now let us see if you have not resolution enough to take it, bad as it is."

The boy hesitatingly took the spoon.

"It is, really, rather baa,' said the gentleman; "but the best way is to summon all your resolution, and down with it at once, like a man."

James made, in reality, a great effort for a child, and swallowed the dose. And who will this child most respect, his deceitful mother, or the honest-dealing stranger? And who will he hereafter most readily believe? It ought, however, to be remarked, that had the child been properly governed, he would at once, and without a murmur, have taken what his mother presented. It is certainly, however, a supposable case, that the child might, after all the arguments of the gentleman, still have refused to do his duty.

What course should then be pursued? Resort to compulsion, but never to deceit. We cannot deceive our children without seriously injuring them, and destroying our own influence. Frank and open dealing is the only safe policy in family government, as well as on the wider theater of life. The underhand arts and cunning maneuvers of the intriguer are sure, in the end, to promote his own overthrow. Be sincere and honest, and you are safe. The only sure way of securing beneficial results, is by virtuous and honorable means.

## Do Not Continually Find Fault with Your Children

It is at times necessary to censure and to punish. But very much more may be done by encouraging children when they do well. Be therefore more careful to express your approbation of good conduct, than your disapprobation of bad. Nothing can more discourage a child than a spirit of incessant faultfinding, on the part of its parent. And hardly anything can exert a more injurious influence upon the disposition both of the parent and the child. There are two great motives influencing human actions; hope and fear. Both of these are at times necessary. But who would not prefer to have her child influenced to good conduct by the desire of pleasing, rather than by the fear of offending.

If a mother never expresses her gratification when her children do well, and is always censuring them when she sees anything amiss, they are discouraged and unhappy. They feel that it is useless to try to please. Their dispositions become hardened and soured by this ceaseless fretting; and at last, finding that, whether they do well or ill, they are equally found fault with, they relinquish all efforts to please, and become heedless of reproaches.

But let a mother approve of her child's conduct whenever she can. Let her show that his good behavior makes her sincerely happy. Let her reward him for his efforts to please, by smiles and affection. In this way she will cherish in her child's heart some of the noblest and most desirable feelings of our nature. She will cultivate in him an amiable disposition and a cheerful spirit. Your child has been, during the day, very pleasant and obedient. Just before putting him to sleep for the night, you take his hand and say, "My son, you have been a very good boy to-day. It makes me very happy to see you so kind and obedient. God loves children who are dutiful to their parents, and he promises to make them happy."

This approbation from, his mother is, to him, a great reward. And when, with a more than ordinarily affectionate tone, you say, "Good night, my dear son," he leaves the room with his little heart full of feeling. And when he closes his eyes for sleep, he is happy, and resolves that he will always try to do his duty.

Basil Hall thus describes the effects produced on board ship, by the different modes of government adopted by different commanders. "Whenever one of these commanding officers," speaking of a fault-finding captain, " came on board the ship, after an absence of a day or two, and likewise when he made his periodical round of the decks after breakfast, his constant habit was to cast his eye about him, in order to discover what was wrong; to detect the smallest thing that was out of its place; in a word, to find as many grounds for censure as possible This constituted, in his opinion, the best preventive to neglect, on the part of those under his command; and he acted in this crusty way on principle.

The attention of the other officer, on the contrary, appeared to be directed chiefly to those points which he could approve of. For instance, he would stop as he went along, from time to time, and say to the first lieutenant, 'Now, these ropes are very nicely arranged; this mode of stowing the men's bags and mess kits is just as I wish to see it;' while the officer first described would not only pass by these well-arranged things, which had cost hours of labor to put in order, quite unnoticed, but would not be easy till his eye had caught hold of some casual mission which afforded an opening for disapprobation. "

One of these captains would remark to the first lieutenant, as he walked along,' How white and clean you have got the decks to-day! I think you must have been at them all the morning, to have got them into such order.' The other, in similar circumstances, but eager to find fault, would say, even if the decks were as white and clean as drifted snow, ' I wish you would teach these sweepers to clear away that bundle of shakings!' pointing to a bit of rope yarn not half an inch long, left under the truck of a gun. It seemed, in short, as if nothing was more vexatious to one of these officers, than to discover things so correct as to afford him no good opportunity for finding fault" while, to the other, the necessity of censuring really appeared a punishment to himself. "Under the one, accordingly, we all worked with cheerfulness, from a conviction that nothing we did in a proper way would miss approbation.

"But our duty under the other, being performed in fear, seldom went on with much spirit. We had no personal satisfaction in doing these things correctly, from the certainty of getting no commendation. "The great chance, also, of being censured, even in those cases where we had labored most industriously to merit approbation, broke the spring of all generous exertion, and by teaching us to anticipate blame as a matter of course, defeated the very purpose of punishment when it fell upon us.

The case being quite hopeless, the chastisement seldom conduced either to the amendment of an offender, or to the prevention of offenses. But what seemed the oddest thing of all was, that these men were both as kindhearted as could be; or, if there were any difference, the fault-finder was the better natured, and, in matters ot professional, the more indulgent of the two.

"The line of conduct I have described was purely a matter of official system, not at all of feeling. Yet, as it then appeared, and still appears to me, nothing could be more completely erroneous than the snarling method of the one, or more decidedly calculated to do good than the approving style of the other. It has, in fact, always appeared to me an absurdity, to make any real distinction between public and private matters in these respects.

"Nor is there the smallest reason why the same principle of civility, or consideration, or by whatever name that quality be called, by which the feelings of others are consulted, should not modify professional intercourse quite as much as it does that of the freest society, without any risk that the requisite strictness of discipline would be hurt by an attention to good manners.

"The desire of discovering that things are right, and a sincere wish to express our approbation, are habits which, in almost every situation in life, have the best possible effects in practice.

"They are vastly more agreeable certainly to the superior himself, whether he be the colonel of a regiment, the captain of a ship, or the head of a house; for the mere act of approving seldom fails to put a man's thoughts into that pleasant train which predisposes him to be habitually pleased, and this frame of mind alone, essentially helps the propagation of a similar cheerfulness among all those who are about him. It requires, indeed, but a very little experience of soldiers or sailors, children, servants, or any other kind of dependents, or even of companions and superiors, to show that this good-humor, on the part of those whom we wish to influence, is the best possible coadjutor to our schemes of management, whatever these may be."

The judicious bestowal of approbation is of the first importance in promoting obedience, and in cultivating in the bosom of your child affectionate and cheerful feelings. Let your smiles animate your boy's heart, and cheer him on in duty. When he returns from school, with his clothes clean and his countenance happy, reward him with the manifestation of a mother's love. This will be the strongest incentive to neatness and care.

An English gentleman used to encourage his little children to early rising, by calling the one who first made her appearance in the parlor in the morning, Lark. The early riser was addressed by that name during the day. This slight expression of parental approval was found sufficient to call up all the children to the early enjoyment of the morning air. A child often makes a very great effort to do something to merit a smile from its mother. And most bitter tears are frequently shed because parents do not sufficiently sympathize in these feelings.

The enjoyment of many a social circle, and the disposition of many an affectionate child, are spoiled by unceasing complainings.

Some persons get into such a habit of finding fault, that it becomes as natural to them as to breathe. Nothing pleases them. In every action, and in every event, they are searching for something to disapprove. Like venomous reptiles, they have the faculty of extracting poison from the choicest blessings. Children are, very much, creatures of sympathy. They form their characters from those around them. And we must cherish in our own bosoms those virtues we would foster in theirs. If we would give them calm and gentle and friendly feelings, we must first show them, by our own example, how valuable those feelings are.

## Never Punish by Exciting Imaginary Fears

There is something very remarkable in the universal prevalence of superstition. Hardly an individual is to be found, enlightened or unenlightened, who is not, in a greater or less degree, under the influence of these irrational fears. There is, in the very nature of man, a strong susceptibility of impression upon this subject. A ghost story will be listened to with an intensity of interest which hardly anything else can awaken.

Persons having the care of children, not infrequently take advantage of this, and endeavor to amuse them by relating these stories, or to govern them by exciting their fears. It surely is not necessary to argue the impropriety of such a course. Everyone knows how ruinous must be the result. Few parents, however, practice the caution which is necessary to prevent others from filling the minds of their children with superstition. How often do we find persons who retain through life the influence which has thus been exerted upon them in childhood. It becomes to them a real calamity. Much watchfulness is required to preserve the mind from such injuries.

There is a mode of punishment, not infrequent, which is very reprehensible. A child is shut up in the cellar, or in a dark closet. It is thus led to associate ideas of terror with darkness. This effect has sometimes been so powerful, that hardly any motive would induce a child to go alone into a dark room. And sometimes even they fear, after they have retired for sleep, to be left alone without a light, But there is no difficulty in training up children to be as fearless by night as by day. And you can find many who do not even dream of danger in going anywhere about the house in the darkest night.

If you would cultivate this state of mind in your children, it is necessary that you should preserve them from ideas of supernatural appearances, and should never appeal to imaginary fears. Train up your children to be virtuous and fearless. Moral courage is one of the surest safeguards of virtue.

An English writer gives a most appalling account of two instances in which fatal consequences attended the strong excitement of fear. Says he, "I knew in Philadelphia, as fine, and as sprightly, and as intelligent a child as ever was born, made an idiot for life, by being, when about three years old, shut into a dark closet by a maid-servant, in order to terrify it into silence. The thoughtless creature first menaced it with sending it to 'the bad place;' and at last to reduce it to silence, put it into the closet, shut the door, and went out of the room. She went back in a few minutes, and found the child in a fit. It recovered from that, but was for life an idiot.

When the parents, who had been out two days and two nights on a visit of pleasure, came home, they were told that the child had had a fit, but they were not told the cause. The girl, however, who was a neighbor's daughter, being on her deathbed about ten years afterward, could not die in peace without sending for the mother of the child and asking forgiveness of her. Thousands upon thousands of human beings have been deprived of their senses by these and similar means.

"It is not long since that we read, in the newspapers, of a child being absolutely killed—the case occurred at Birmingham, I think—by being thus frightened. The parents had gone out into what is called an evening party. The servants, naturally enough, had their party at home; and the mistress, who, by some unexpected accident, had been brought home at an early hour, finding the parlor full of company, ran up stairs to find her child, which was about two or three years old. She found it with its eyes open, but fixed; touching it, she found it inanimate. 'The doctor was sent for in vain: it was dead. The maid affected to know nothing of the cause; but someone of the parties assembled discovered, pinned up to the curtains of the bed, a horrid figure, made up partly of a frightful mask! This, as the wretched girl confessed, had been done to keep the child quiet while she was with her company below.

When one reflects on the anguish that the poor little thing must have endured before the life was quite frightened out of it, one can find no terms sufficiently strong to express the abhorrence due to the perpetrator of this crime, which was, in fact, a cruel murder; and, if it was beyond the reach of the law, it was so, because, as in the case of parricide, the law in making no provision for wickedness so unnatural, has, out of respect to human nature, supposed such crimes to be impossible."

I have in this chapter alluded to some of the most common and prominent faults in education; They cannot all, however, be particularly mentioned. The faithful mother must have continually a watchful eye; she must observe the effect of her own practices. She must carefully search out every little defect and trifling error. We must think and observe for ourselves. It is vain to hope to make attainment in anything valuable without effort.

The views of others may be of essential aid in laying down general principles, in exciting our own thoughts, and in stimulating us to resolution and fidelity. But after all, unless we are willing to think, ourselves; to study the dispositions of our children; to watch the influence of the various motives which we present to their minds, many faults will pass undetected, and we shall lose many advantages that we might otherwise have obtained.

# 6

## Methods and Plans

IN the government of a family, and in the moral and intellectual training of children, there is room for the exercise of a great deal of ingenuity in the formation of plans for the accomplishment of the objects intended, by means more "or less indirect, but not the less efficient on that account. I will in this chapter describe some plans of this character by way of illustration of my meaning.

### The Black Book

The Black Book. The following plan was once adopted by a gentleman, who was to be absent from home for a week or two, with his wife, leaving two or three children under the care of an The evening before they went, the gentleman made a small blank book with a thick paper cover. Upon the cover, he made a broad black stripe, and wrote the words BLACK BOOK in capitals. On the first leaf inside the book, he wrote the following:—

"DIRECTIONS.

"When either of the children is guilty of any act of disobedience, neglect of duty, insubordination, or contention, or of any other offense, they are to make an entry of the case in this book, at

Aunt Maria's direction. If they are ill-humored and sullen about it, then Aunt Maria is to make the entry herself, stating the reason why the guilty one did not do it. If, when I come home, I find this book empty, I shall fear that Aunt Maria has not been faithful."

When the gentleman returned from his journey, he found the following entries made by his children:—

"To-day James had two recesses, and I was cross about it, and went down stairs before it was time and said it was not right that he should have two recesses and I only one. And he told Aunt Maria that he ought not to have had but one. MARY."

"This morning when Aunt Maria was correcting my French, I played; I laid down upon the sofa two or three times, and played with some pens and books, though she asked me not to do so, repeatedly. JAMES."

"To-day when we were coming home from a visit James and I had a difficulty. I told Aunt Maria something that I did not wish James to know, but he kept teasing me all the time about it; so I kept telling him to keep still, and told him not to trouble me; and I felt very unpleasantly about it. MARY."

"Yesterday morning when I was getting ready to go to Mr. J.'s to make a visit I made Aunt Maria some difficulty. I kept calling her when she could not come, and made some difficulty about my clothes and other things. JAMES."

"This morning Mary came to my desk and took a slate-pencil out of it. I thought she was going to take it away to use, which I thought was wrong, so I told her to go and get her own, and not meddle with my things. JAMES."

## THE MOTHER AT HOME

"This afternoon when Mary was swinging, standing up, I went and stood before her. When I did this, she said, 'Stay there, and you will get it presently.' When she came up to me I struck her pretty hard on her foot. Then she said, ' Oh, James! oh, James!' Then I stopped the swing, and she said that I almost pushed her out. JAMES."

"This morning when Aunt Maria had corrected my French, she told me to go to my lessons, but I did not go. I said that I must put away a newspaper first, then she told me again to go, and I put down the newspaper and went, and sat down at my desk, but instead of studying, I began to tell Mary the French names of the days of the week. Then Aunt Maria told me to put it down in the black book for disobedience. JAMES."

"Just now, when we were singing, I lent my book to Aunt Maria, and when I went to get it again, Mary took my place. When I came back I told her to let me have my place, but she told me she should keep it because she wanted to look over. Then I went and asked Aunt Maria if Mary must not let me have my place. At first she said yes, but afterward said that I must change places with her. Then I looked cross and would not sing. JAMES."

"Yesterday Mary was sitting in mother's low rocking-chair, and I took a rope and tied one of her arms up to the chair, and tied the other with a piece of white string to another part of the chair. Then Aunt Maria told me she wanted me to go away of an errand to get a dress. Then I asked Mary if she would untie herself while I was gone, but she did not answer, then I asked her again, but she did not answer, so I struck her. Then Aunt Maria told me that I must put it down in the black book. JAMES."

"Just now when I had learned my Latin lesson I spoke to George, though it was study hours, (for our doors were open) to know how many sheets of paper a large fire-balloon, which they sent up last night at the Museum, was made of, but he did not hear me, so I asked him again. But before he could answer, Aunt Maria came up and told me to put it down here. JAMES."

"Yesterday when I was throwing sticks at John Harmer, in the street, Nancy told me not to do it, but I kept on throwing them, and told Nancy it would not be her fault if I hit him, and that I wished she would go home. Another time I was rolling marbles on the kitchen floor, and went to one side of the floor to see if I could make them go across. Nancy told me not to do so, but I told her that the kitchen was as much mine as hers, and that I thought she was very cross. This morning Aunt Maria told me to put it down here; and she told me that if I would ask Nancy to forgive me, I might put that down too, so I did. JAMES."

It is very desirable in all government to avoid the infliction of disgrace. When a child loses his self-respect, and feels dishonored, one of the strongest motives to correct conduct is lost. If a child can be induced good-naturedly, and yet justly to pronounce sentence upon his own conduct, a very powerful influence is brought to bear upon the mind, which is salutary in the highest degree.

The plan above described, therefore, must have exerted a powerful, and at the same time a genial and kindly effect upon the hearts of the children who made the entries.

## Children's Journals

There can be, in fact, no better plan, in family government, than to induce the children to keep a journal in which they shall record such things which they may do that are wrong, as the parent may think that this mode of discipline is adapted to remedy.

For those children of a family who have sufficient age and maturity of mind, the plan of writing a full and regular journal of whatever interests and concerns them, and especially of all that relates to their intellectual and moral progress, may well be recommended. Such a journal may assume a great variety of forms. It may be a religious diary. It may be a narrative of personal incidents. It may be a record of resolutions made, with an account subsequently of the manner in which they have been kept. Or it may consist of all these combined.

Even very young children can keep such journals, with a little help and encouragement from the mother. The work must however be managed in such a way as not to be a burden to them. They must not be expected to write too much, or too frequently, or at unseasonable times, when their minds are interested in other things.

Older children who may attempt such an exercise will be much aided by reading the celebrated essay of John Foster upon one writing memoirs of one's self. He recommends earnestly to everyone, who would become acquainted with his own heart, or who would attain to excellence of character, to review the path that he has trod in life's pilgrimage, and to record those influences which have guided him this way or that on his journey. No one can thus seriously retrace his steps, without being profoundly impressed with a sense of the dangers he has escaped, of the errors and sins into which he has fallen, and of the goodness of God, in rescuing him from so many perils. There can hardly be a more excellent, intellectual, and moral exercise, for one who has attained maturity of mind, than thus to review the past.

Louis Philippe, the late King of the French, was, in early life placed under the tuition of Madame de Genlis. She taught her pupil to examine his mind and regulate his character by keeping a very minute daily journal. This daily examination was conducted with great fidelity, as the following questions which he every evening answered will testify.

1. Have I this day fulfilled all my duties toward God, my Creator, and prayed to Him with fervor and affection?
2. Have I listened with respect and attention to the instructions which have been given me, with regard to my Christian duties, and to the reading of works of piety?
3. Have I fulfilled all my duties this day toward those I ought to love most in the world, my father and my mother?
4. Have I behaved with mildness and kindness toward my sister and my brothers?
5. Have I been docile, grateful, and attentive to my teachers?
6. Have I been perfectly sincere to-day, disobeying no one, and speaking evil of no one? 7 Have 1 been as discreet, prudent, charitable, modest, and courageous as may be expected at my age?
7. Have I shown no proof of that weakness and effeminacy which is so contemptible in a man?
8. Have I done all the good I could?
9. Have I shown all the marks of attention I ought to the persons absent or present, to whom I owe kindness, respect, and affection?

Every evening these questions were read to Louis Philippe by his teacher, and he returned an answer to each in his journal. This exercise was followed by a season of devotion, in which the young prince sought of God the pardon of his errors, and implored Divine grace and assistance for the future.

This was the moral and intellectual training of a youth of sixteen. In the midst of the most voluptuous court of Europe, surrounded by the most dazzling allurements of gilded vice, with the notorious Duke of Orleans for his father—young, sanguine, rich, and of exalted birth, protected by this discipline, he moved uncontaminated through all these dangerous scenes, and through all the temptations and vicissitudes of half a century, sustained a character of the most irreproachable and the purest morality.

The influence of such training must be powerful in the extreme.

It is hardly possible for any young person thus to review at the close of the day his feelings and his conduct, especially if such a review be connected with confession and prayer, without becoming firmly established in correct principles. Punishment of any kind could hardly be required in a family where this course was faithfully pursued, by a judicious parent.

It is said that the distinguished statesman, John Quincy Adams, amid all the pressure of one of the busiest lives through which man ever passed, found time during the whole period of his life, to keep a journal of all the important events of each day. This journal extended at last to upward of seventy thick quarto volumes. And it was probably to this, more than to any other cause, that he was indebted, for that almost miraculous amount of information with which his mind was stored.

## Mother's Journals

Besides the journals which children themselves may write, the mother may derive great advantage sometimes from keeping a record of the progress of her children, and the general history of her family. I knew a mother who kept a constant journal of the progress of a beloved child from his earliest infancy. She carefully noted down her more important acts of discipline, and observed the effect which her course produced upon the character of her child. With more solicitude and vigilance than the physician watches the effect of his prescriptions, did she watch the effect of her moral remedies and antidotes. His opening faculties, the developments of his affections, his constitutional temperament, his prominent foibles, were made the subject of continued deliberation. They were committed to writing. Thus was this mother gaining information more rapidly than she could possibly gain it in any other way. She was accustoming her own mind to independent investigation and thought. Every day she was gaining knowledge of the effect of different motives upon the mind. And her influence over her child was every day increasing. Now this looks like maternal fidelity. It shows that the mother feels her need of information, and is anxious to acquire it. And it shows that she is willing to make intellectual effort herself, that she may be able to discharge her duties.

Let a mother adopt such a course as this, and she must be most rapidly advancing in knowledge of the art of guiding the youthful mind. When her child first manifests irritation, let her write down the course she pursued to allay that irritation, and the success which attended her efforts.

I will give a specimen of what I suppose would be the general character of such a journal.

> Jan. 10, 1833. To-day Charles became very angry with his sister, and pushed her down. As a punishment, I gave Mary an apple, and gave Charles none. But I thought Charles seemed, instead of being subdued, to be made envious by it, and more vexed with his sister than before.

> Jan. 15, 1833. Mary to-day treated her brother unkindly. I thought I would try a different course from that which I pursued with Charles. I called them both to me and said, ' Mary, God is displeased when he sees you indulging such feelings. And now how can you ask God tonight to take care of you, when you have been disobeying him today?' Having talked with her a little while in this strain, she burst into tears, and asked her brother's forgiveness. They were soon playing again, as happy and as affectionate as ever. Before Mary went to sleep tonight she asked God's forgiveness, and promised that she would try never to be angry again. I cannot but hope that an impression was produced upon both their minds, which will not soon be forgotten.

Jan 18, 1833. Charles to-day accidentally broke a valuable lamp. I fear that I unjustly blamed him. I must endeavor to have my feelings under more perfect control.

Jan 22, 1833. Mary is beginning to manifest improper fondness for dress. We have had much company lately, and many have spoken to her about her beautiful gown. I must dress her in such a manner that she will not attract attention."

If some such course as this is pursued with perseverance, great skill will certainly be acquired in the art of governing. The mother must in some way or other direct the energies of her own mind to this subject. She must watch the peculiarities of the dispositions of her children. She must think and experiment for herself.

After writing the above, the following communication was placed in my hand. As it was written by a mother who has long practiced upon the plan here recommended, and who, from her numerous cares might, with more propriety than almost any other parent, claim exemption from this duty, I with great pleasure insert it. It is the testimony of successful experiment.

"Perhaps to some mothers it may at first appear impossible to carry on, with any degree of system or accuracy, anything like a regular journal. It is true, that it would at first require some effort; but if it would aid a mother in discharging her duties, where is the conscientious parent who would shrink from such an effort? There are many benefits to be expected from such a record, and it should perhaps be merely a record or note-book, that it may not encroach too much upon the time, especially in the case of those mothers who are obliged to employ a great proportion of their time in attending to the domestic duties of their families.

The first benefit resulting to the mother herself, would be the necessity of making some regular mental effort. A young mother, surrounded with family cares and duties, may feel at first as if she had no time for mental and intellectual labor; but ten minutes every day devoted to such a purpose, would soon convince her that her other duties are probably the better performed for such a diary. Her duties to her children certainly will not be attended to with less interest; and she is gradually fitting herself, by such discipline, however trifling, to be their teacher and guide.

The habit of keeping such memoranda also induces a mother to look with greater scrutiny into her own motives of action, into her principles of family government, and to govern her own heart and conduct, and to cultivate more of a spirit which every mother needs—a spirit of prayer.

I am confident that, would mothers do this, mutual benefit and assistance would be given to that class of society to whom we must look for much of the future happiness of the community. And many a young parent would feel her hand strengthened and her heart lightened in the cause of infant instruction.

The plan which I would suggest might be something like the following.

1. Notice the earliest developments of temper in your child, and give the result of simple experiments made to subdue and conquer
2. Remark what things peculiarly interest your child, and describe how you improve the opportunity of giving the child a moral and religious lesson drawn from the object of interest. Show the effect and result of such an
3. Describe the course pursued to insure obedience. State the difficulties which you encountered, and how they were overcome.
4. Describe the course of first religious instruction, and what generally excites the strongest interest in your child's mind.

In this way you may assist many a trembling mother in doing her duty; and the result of an experience which perhaps it costs you but a few minutes of time to throw into a suitable form on paper, will, through the pages of some religious magazine, be circulated to the farthest parts of our country, and be exerting a powerful influence on the hearts of mothers—an inestimable one on the prospects, both for time and eternity, of the rising generation."

The following is an extract from such a notebook, kept by a mother, and written without any reference to its insertion here.

Perhaps there are few dispositions which require more judicious, firm, and steady management, in a child, than that which is often ranked under obstinacy or stubbornness. There is certainly no fault, which, if neglected, or allowed to gain strength, is more likely to bring down the heart of a parent with sorrow to the grave, and to insure to the child a youth and manhood of wretchedness. It grows with the growth, and strengthens with the strength. Yet I have heard more than one mother say, ' That child is very obstinate; he will have his own way, and I suppose he is too young to understand now, and frequent punishment only hardens the heart.'

A child cannot be too young to learn; that is, as soon as a child begins to notice and watch the tones of the voice and the expression of the countenance, it is of an age to receive moral lessons. It is undoubtedly true, that in administering punishment, care should be taken to do it in such a way that it shall tend to soften and subdue the heart, not irritate it. Yet the child must be made to feel that its spirit must yield to paternal authority. For instance, your child is playing with some forbidden article. You direct him, gently, but firmly, to put it down—he refuses. If you rise and take it by force, the child cries—he is vexed and disappointed. Instead of this, if you say, pointing to the article, ' You must put it down,' and he refuses, a second command in the voice of seriousness and authority will seldom fail of insuring obedience.

The child should then see an approving look or smile, and if taken up and amused by something which you are sure will interest him, he will not forget the lesson, particularly if pains is taken to associate the forbidden thing with something which gives him a sensation of pleasure. Return to it and say, 'You must not touch that; no, no,' and repeat it two or three times. Then give the child something which is not so familiar as to be worthless, and say, ' You may have this.' A child often or twelve months may soon be taught, in this way, distinct lessons of obedience.

If it refuses to yield, some slight punishment should be inflicted, which shall connect the idea of bodily suffering or inconvenience: but care should be afterward taken to interest the child, and your countenance should evince no anger or irritability.

A child of less than three years was often troublesome to his mother, through an unyielding disposition which he manifested. He had been severely punished for his fault, though never unless the danger of omitting the punishment made the risk to the child's future happiness very great. Once, after a very decided case of obstinacy had occurred, it became necessary to punish him. After it was over, he said he was not sorry for the fault. He had never been shut up in the dark, as a punishment, because with very young children the consequences of such a measure are sometimes hazardous; but it was known that in this case the child was not afraid; and I desired to know the effect of it, in connection with religious considerations. The following experiment was tried, and the conversation is here precisely as it occurred.

> Mother: "I am sorry you are so naughty. I must put you into a dark closet, where nobody can see you."
>
> Child. Speaking very deliberately: "I don't want to get up and be good."
>
> Mother: "When you are a good boy, you may call me, and I will open the door; but till then you must be quiet, and not touch anything.'

He remained perfectly still more than ten minutes, then knocked loudly on the door.

> Mother: "Are you good now?"

Child: "Not if I come out there."

Mother: "What are you knocking for?"

Child: "I want to get out."

Mother: :If you are good, I will open the door; but you have been very naughty, and troubled me. Are you going to be good?"

Child: "No; I ain't good and sorry—I don't want to come out."

Mother" "I am very sorry that my little boy is naughty. He is in the closet, where it is very dark, and Mother cannot see him, but God can see him. God is displeased with you. I want you to think of that. Can you think of God, and ask him to take care of you, while you are so cross and ill-humored?"

He was still for about a minute, and then said, in a pleasant subdued tone, "I am good now, mamma." He came out, made every proper concession and acknowledgment, and then went to his play, as if nothing had occurred to disturb his tranquility. I have not the least doubt that this occurrence will have a strong and lasting impression, and save a mother's heart many a pang in time to come, and prevent the necessity of severe punishment."

There is an impression upon the minds of many persons, that skill in governing must be instinctive; that it is an original and native talent, and not to be acquired by information or thought. But look at those parents who have been most successful in family government, and they will be found to be those who have most diligently and uniformly attended to the subject. You may go into the family of some man of celebrity, in one of the learned professions, and, as you look upon his lawless children, you are perhaps discouraged. You say, if this man, with his powerful and highly cultivated mind, cannot succeed in family government, how can I expect success? But a little observation will satisfy you that this man is giving his time and attention to other pursuits. He is neglecting his children, and they are forming precisely such characters as we should expect from the influences to which they are exposed.

No course of procedure, without the blessing of God, will result in the piety of the child. But if we go on in our attempts to govern without system, or thought, or care, we shall undoubtedly reap most bitter consequences. The mother must study her duty. She must carefully observe the effect produced by her mode of discipline. There is but little advantage to be derived from books, unless we revolve their contents in our own minds. Others may suggest the most valuable ideas. But we must take those ideas and dwell upon them, and trace out their effects, and incorporate them into our own minds by associating them with others of our own. We must accustom ourselves to investigation and thought. The mother who will do this, will most certainly grow in wisdom. She will daily perceive that she is acquiring more facility in forming in her child the character she desires. And the increasing obedience and affection that she will receive, will be her constant reward. Care and labor are necessary in training up a family. But no other cares are rewarded with so rich a recompense; no other labors insure such permanent and real enjoyment. You, O mothers, have immortal souls entrusted to your keeping. Their destiny is in a great degree in your hands. Your ignorance or unfaithfulness may be the means of sinking them to the world of woe. Your fidelity, by the blessing of God, may elevate them to the mansions of heaven. You and your children may soon be ranging with angel wings to realms of blest spirits, if, here, you are faithful in prayer and effort to train them up for heaven.

# 7

# Religious Instruction

IN the religious instruction of children the following important principles must be kept in mind:

## Make the Training of Your Children Your Own Personal Duty

Parents must make the religious training of their children their own personal duty. Very great success has attended the efforts which have been made to collect children in Sabbath schools for religious instruction. Maternal associations have been of inestimable value. But nothing can supersede the necessity of effort and instruction at the fireside. The mother must collect her little flock around her and take upon herself the responsibility of their religious education. She may find enjoyment and improvement in associating with others for prayer; and if she be faithful, she will see that her children are punctual attendants of the Sabbath school. But she will not regard these as exonerating herself in the least degree from responsibility.

The influence of Sabbath-schools has undoubtedly tended to awaken more general interest at home in behalf of the spiritual welfare of children. Still there is danger that some parents may feel that the responsibility is transferred from themselves to the Sabbath-school teachers; and that they accomplish their duty in seeing that their children are punctually at school with their lessons well committed. It is, however, of the first importance that home should be the sanctuary of religious instruction. The mother must be the earnest and affectionate guide to the Savior. She must take her little ones by the hand and lead them in the paths of piety.

No one else can possibly have the influence which a mother may possess, or the facilities which she enjoys. She knows the various dispositions of her children; their habits of thought; their moods of mind. Thus can she adapt instruction to their wants. She alone can improve the numberless occurrences which open the mind for instruction, and give it susceptibility to religious impression. She is with them when they are in sickness or pain. She can take advantage of the calm of the morning, and of the solemn stillness of the evening.

In moments of sadness she can point their minds to brighter worlds, and to more satisfying joys. God has conferred upon the mother advantages which no one else can possess. With these advantages he has connected responsibilities which cannot be laid aside, or transferred to another. It is at home, therefore, and by the parents, that the great duty of religious education must be chiefly performed. The quiet fireside is the most sacred sanctuary; maternal affection is the most eloquent pleader, and an obedient child is the most promising subject of religious impressions. Let mothers feel this as they ought, and they will seldom see their children leave the paternal roof with their hearts unfortified with Christian principles and sincere piety.

## Parents Must Have Deep Devotional Feelings Themselves

It is certainly vain to hope that you can induce your children to fix their affections upon another world, while yours are fixed upon this. Your example in such a case will counteract all the influence of your instructions. Unless Christian feelings animate your heart, it is folly to expect that you can instill those principles into the hearts of your children. They will imitate your example. They confide in your guidance.

That little child which God has given you, and which is so happy in your affection, feels safe in cherishing those feelings which it sees that you are cherishing. And, mother! can you look upon your confiding child and witness all her fond endearments and warm embraces, and not feel remorse in the consciousness that your example is leading her away from God, and consigning her to ceaseless sorrow?

You love your child. Your child loves you, and cannot dream that you are abusing its confidence, and leading it in the paths of sin and destruction. How would it be shocked in being told that its mother is the cruel betrayer of its eternal happiness! You are wedded to the world. You have not given your heart to God. Not content with being the destroyer of your own soul, you must carry with you to the world of woe, the child who is loving you as its mother .and its friend. O there is an aggravation of cruelty in this which cannot be described.

One would think that every smile which you see upon the face of your child would disturb your peace; that every proof of its affection would pierce your heart; that remorse would keep you awake at midnight, and embitter every hour. The murderer of the body can scarce withstand the stings of conscience. But, O unchristian mother! you are the destroyer of the soul. And of whose soul? The soul of your own confiding child.

We cannot speak less plainly on this topic. We plead the unparalleled wrongs of children, betrayed by a mother's smile and a mother's kiss. Satan led Adam from Paradise. Judas betrayed his Master. But here we see a mother leading her child, her own immortal child, far from God and peace, to the rebellion of worldliness and the storms of retribution. That little child following in your footsteps, is the heir of eternity. It is to survive the lapse of all coming years; to emerge from the corruptions of the grave; to expand in spiritual existence, soaring in the angel's lofty flight, or groping in the demon's gloom. Thou, O mother! art its guide to immortality; to heaven's green pastures, or to the dreary wastes of despair. If you go on in impenitence and sin, your child, in all probability, will go with you.

We have heard of a child, upon her dying bed, raising her eyes to her parents and exclaiming, in bitterness of spirit, " O my parents! you never told me of death, or urged me to prepare for it; and now," said she, bursting into an agony of tears, " I am dying, and my soul is lost." She died. Her sun went down in darkness.

What were the feelings of those parents! What agony must have rent their bosoms! How must the specter of their ruined daughter have pursued them in all the employments of the day, and disturbed their slumbers by night. Remember that though you should be separated from your children by death, you must meet them again. The trump of judgment will summon you to the bar of Christ. How fruitless would be the attempt to describe your feelings there, if it should prove that you had been their destroyer. ,

"That awful day will surely come; The appointed hour makes haste."

Death is succeeded by judgment, and judgment by eternity. If you are the destroyer of your child, the consequences will be eternal. If you had been faithful, yourself and your child might have been reposing in heaven.

Think not you can go in one path, and induce your child to walk in another. You must not only "point to heaven," but "lead the way." The first thing to be done, is for a mother to give her own heart to God. Become a Christian yourself, and then you may hope for God's blessing upon your efforts to lead your child to the Savior.

We do entreat every mother who reads these pages, as she values her own happiness and the happiness-of her children, immediately to surrender her heart to God. Atoning blood has removed every difficulty from the way. The Holy Spirit is ready, in answer to your prayers, to grant you all needful assistance. Every hour that you neglect this duty, you are leading your children farther from God, and rendering the prospect of their return more hopeless.

It is in vain to expect that you can do anything effectual to win the soul of your child to God, without possessing sincere piety yourself. The mother who endeavors to impress her children with a feeling of gratitude to God, because she coldly thinks it her duty, will fail. Instead of gratitude, she will excite only weariness and loathing. But if the feeling itself glows in her heart, it will readily kindle up in theirs. Perhaps some of the parents who may read this volume are unreconciled to God themselves. They have children whom they are commanded to bring up to piety. If sincere and devoted piety in the parent is an indispensable requisite, what shall they do? It is a hard question—a very hard case. An individual is placed in this world of probation, and God says to him or to her, " Come, and be mine, and in a few years I will call you to a home of perpetual peace and happiness."

The beings thus invited hesitate— look upon the world—upon heaven—linger a little, and then decide against God, and begin to walk deliberately on in the downward road. They have proceeded for some distance on this awful descent, when a helpless dependent one is committed to their care. They take him by the hand, and lead him on. He knows not whither he is going. He loves his parents— confides in them—and believes fully that they cannot lead him into any danger.

He clings, therefore, closely to them, and walks heedlessly on. But the parents feel not entirety at ease; a mother cannot, under such circumstances, if she at all understands the case. They accordingly hesitate a moment in their course, and then try to send back their child. They give it religious instruction—they teach it the Bible, and send it to the Sabbath-school, in hopes that it will be prevailed upon to return, while they go forward in the road to ruin. What madness! Seek God yourself, and your child may perhaps accompany you. But you cannot expect that he will enter the "strait gate," while you are going on in the broad way.

JOHN S. C. ABBOTT

## Present Religion in a Pleasant Way

Present religion in a pleasant aspect. There is no real enjoyment without piety. The tendency of religion is to make us happy here and hereafter; to divest the mind of gloom, and fill it with joy. Many parents err in this respect. They dwell too much upon the terrors of the law. They speak with countenances saddened and gloomy.

Religion becomes to the child an unwelcome topic, and is regarded as destructive of happiness. The idea of God is associated with gloom and terror. Many parents have, in their latter years, become convinced of the injudiciousness of the course that they have pursued in this respect—finding that they have so connected religious considerations with melancholy countenances and mournful tones of voice, as to cause the subject to be unnecessarily repugnant.

We may, indeed, err upon the other extreme. The nature of sin, and the justice of God, and the awful penalty of his law, should be distinctly exhibited. The child should be taught to regard God as a being who, while he loves his creatures, cannot look upon sin but with abhorrence. If we speak to children simply of the Creator's goodness, as manifested in the favors we are daily receiving, an erroneous impression of God's character will be conveyed. It is to be feared that many deceive themselves in thinking that they love God. They have in their minds a poetic idea of an amiable and sentimental being, whose character is composed of fondness and indulgence.

Such persons are as far from worshiping the true God, as is the Indian devotee or the sensual Moslem. God must be represented as he has exhibited himself to us in the Bible and in the works of nature. He is a God of mercy and of justice. He is a God of love; and he is also a consuming fire. He is to be regarded with our warmest affection, and also with reverence and godly fear. Let, therefore, children distinctly understand that sin cannot pass unpunished. But they should also understand that judgment is God's strange work. Ordinarily speak of his goodness. Show his readiness to forgive.

Excite the gratitude of the child by speaking of the joys of heaven. Thus let the duties of religion ever be connected with feelings of enjoyment and images of happiness, that the child may perceive that gloom and sorrow are connected only with disobedience and irreligion. There is enough in the promised joys of heaven to rouse a child's most animated feelings. This subject has more to cheer the youthful heart than any other which can be presented. Appeal to gratitude. Excite hope. Speak of the promised reward. Thus may you most reasonably hope to lead your child to love its Maker, and to live for heaven. Reserve the terrors of the law for solemn occasions, when you may produce a deep and abiding impression. If you are continually introducing these motives, the mind becomes hardened against their influence; religion becomes a disagreeable topic, and the inveteracy of sin is confirmed.

Besides its influence upon the minds of our children, the effect upon our own minds of taking cheerful views of the providence and government of God will be most salutary. We must at all times remember that promotion of happiness, is the great object which God has in view in all his operations. For this he made men free; for this he gave his law. Every sorrow which is sent to the human heart is sent in love, to promote real and permanent enjoyment. God never willingly afflicts. When the heart is crushed with the heaviest weight of suffering, the voice of God declares, that this suffering is the means which he is using, to banish sorrow forever, and to fill the heart with joy. Yes! God loves happiness, and is employed at all times and in every part of the universe, in adopting those plans which to him seem most effectual for the fulfillment of his benevolent designs.

## Improve Appropriate Occasions

We all know that with every child there are times when we find in them a peculiar tenderness of conscience and susceptibility of impression. Changes of mood in fact come over the minds of all, and sometimes from unaccountable causes. One day the Christian will feel a warmth of devotional feeling and elevation of spiritual enjoyment, which the next day he in vain endeavors to attain.

The man whose affections are fixed upon the world, at one time will be almost satisfied with the pleasures that he is gathering. The world looks bright; hope is animated; and he rushes on with new vigor in his delusive pursuits. The next day all his objects of desire appear like perfect shadows. He feels the heartlessness of his pleasures; his spirit is sad within him; and he is almost resolved to be a Christian. With these changes nearly all are familiar. Sometimes they may be accounted for from known external causes. At other times the causes elude our search.

A mother should ever be watchful to improve such occasions. When she sees her child with an unusually tender spirit, with a pensive countenance and subdued feelings—let her then look to God in fervent prayer, and with all the persuasions of a mother's love endeavor to guide her child to the Savior. When the mind is in such a state as this, it is prepared for religious instruction. It then can be made to feel how heartless are all joys but those of piety. Its hold upon the world is loosened, and it may more easily be led to wander in those illimitable regions where it may hereafter find its home.

O how sweet a pleasure it is to present the joys of religion to a child whose feelings are thus chastened; to behold the tear of feeling moistening its eye; to see its little bosom heaving with the new emotions which are rising there! If there be a joy on earth, it is to be found in such a scene as this. The happy mother thus guiding the young immortal to its heavenly home, experiences a rapture of feeling which the world knoweth not of. Such occasions are not infrequently arising, and the mother should endeavor always to have her heart warm with love to Christ, that in such an hour she may communicate the warmth of this affection to the bosom of her child.

There are certain seasons also which are peculiarly appropriate for guiding the thoughts to heaven. Our feelings vary with scenes around us. Upon some dark and tempestuous night you lead your little son to his chamber. The rain beats violently upon the windows. The wind whistles around the corners of the dwelling. All without is darkness and gloom. The mind of the child is necessarily affected by this rage of the elements. You embrace the opportunity to inculcate a lesson of trust in God.

"My son," you say, "it is God who causes this wind to blow, and the rain to fall. Neither your father nor I can make the storm cease, or increase its violence. If God wished to do so, he could cause the wind to blow with such fury as to beat in all the windows and destroy the house. But God will take care of you, my son, if you sincerely ask him. No one else can take care of you. I hope that you will pray that God will protect you, and your father, and me, tonight. When God commands, the storm will cease. The clouds will disappear; all will be calm. And the bright moon and twinkling stars will shine out again."

In some such manner as this the child may be taught his entire dependence upon God. And under such instructions he cannot fail of obtaining a deep impression of the power of his Maker. You may say that God is omnipotent, and it will produce but a feeble impression. But point to some actual exhibition of God's power, and the attention is arrested, and the truth is felt. When the mother leaves the room, and her son remains alone and in darkness, listening to the roar of the storm, will not his mind be expanded with new ideas of the greatness and the power of his Maker? Will he not feel that it is a fearful thing to offend such a being? And if he has been rightly instructed to place his trust in God, the agitation of the elements will not trouble the serenity of his heart. He will feel that with God for his protector, he need fear no evil. Some such simple occurrence as this may often be improved to produce an impression which never can be forgotten.

Such thoughts as these, introduced to the mind of a child, will enlarge its capacities, give it maturity, lead it to reflection, and, by the blessing of God, promote its eternal well-being. One such transient incident has a greater effect than hours of ordinary religious conversation.

One of the most important duties of the mother is to watch for such occasions and diligently to improve them. Any parent who is faithful will find innumerable opportunities which will enable her to come into almost immediate contact with the heart of her child. The hour of sickness comes. Your little daughter is feverish and restless upon her pillow. You bathe her burning brow and moisten her parched tongue, and she hears your prayer that she may be restored to health. At length the fever subsides. She awakes from refreshing sleep, relieved from pain. You tell her then, that if God had not interposed, her sickness would have increased till she had died. By pointing her attention to this one act of kindness in God, which she can see and feel, you may excite emotions of sincere gratitude. You may thus lead her to real grief that she should ever disobey her heavenly Father.

A child in the neighborhood dies. Your daughter accompanies you to the funeral. She looks upon the lifeless corpse of her little companion. And shall a mother neglect such an opportunity to teach her child the meaning of death? When your daughter retires to sleep at night, she will most certainly think of her friend who has died. As you speak to her of eternity and the judgment-seat of Christ—will not her youthful heart feel? And will not tears of sympathy fill her eyes? And as you tell your daughter that she too soon must die and appear before Christ to be judged, will not the occurrence of the day give a reality and an effect to your remarks which will long be remembered?

There are few children who can resist such appeals. The Savior, who took little children in his arms and blessed them, will not despise this day of small things, but will cherish the feelings thus excited, and strengthen the feeble resolve. We have every encouragement to believe that God, who is more ready to give his Holy Spirit to them that ask him, than a mother to feed her hungry child, will accompany these efforts with his blessing. A father once led his little daughter into the graveyard, to show her the grave of a playmate, who, a few days before, had been consigned to her cold and narrow bed. The little girl looked for some moments in silence and sadness upon the fresh mound, and then looking up, said, "Papa, I now know what is meant by the hymn,

'I, in the burying-place, may see,
Graves shorter there than I.'
"My grave would be longer than this."

This dear little child now lies by the side of that grave. But her parents can smile through their tears, as they hold on to the blessed hope of heaven. It is by introducing children to such scenes, and seizing upon such occasions, that we may most successfully inculcate lessons of piety. One such incident enters more deeply into the heart than volumes of ordinary conversation.

You are perhaps riding with your son. It is a lovely summer's morning. The fields lie spread before you in beauty. The song of the bird is heard. All nature seems uttering a voice of gladness. As you ascend some eminence which gives you a commanding view of all the varied beauties of the scene; of hill and valley, rivulet and forest, of verdant pastures and lowing herds, can you fail to point the attention of your son to these beauties, an 1 from them to lead his mind to Him whose word called them all into being? May you not thus most effectually carry his thoughts away to heaven? May you not lead his mind to the green pastures and the still waters, where there is sweet repose forever? May you not introduce him to that kind Shepherd, who there protects his flock, gathering his lambs in his aims, and folding them in his bosom? May not a mother's or a father's tongue here plead with an eloquence unknown in the pulpit?

By carefully improving such occasions as these, you may produce an impression upon the mind, which all future years cannot remove. You may so intimately connect devotional feelings with the ever-varying events and changing scenes of life, that every day's occurrences will lead the thoughts of your child to God.

The raging storm; the hour of sickness; the funeral procession; the tolling bell, will, in all after-life, carry back his thoughts to a mother's instructions and prayers. Should your son hereafter be a wanderer from home, as he stands upon the Alps, or rides upon the ocean, his mind will involuntarily be carried to Him who rules the waters and who built the hills. With all those occasions then, which produce so vivid an effect upon the mind, endeavor to connect views of God and heaven.

I can never forget the impression produced upon my own mind by a very simple remark, which, under ordinary circumstances, would not have been remembered an hour. It affords so good an illustration of the principle which we are now considering, as to overcome the reluctance which I feel in appealing to personal experience. One day, in the very early stages of my childhood, my father gave me a little ball covered with leather, such as boys usually play with. Saturday morning, while playing with it at school, it was accidentally thrown over the fence and lost. We searched for it a long time in vain. The loss to me was as severe as it would be for a man to part with half his fortune. I went home and un-bosomed my grief to my mother. She endeavored to console me, but with what effect I cannot now remember. The next day was the Sabbath. I passed the day with more than ordinary propriety.

My customary Sabbath hymn was perfectly committed. Seated in my little chair by the fire, I passed a quiet and happy day in reading, and in the various duties appropriate to holy time. My conduct was such as to draw expressions of approbation from my parents, as with a peaceful heart I bade them good night, to retire to rest. The next day, as usual, I went to school. The lost ball occupied my mind as I walked along.

Upon climbing over the fence into the field where I had so long and so fruitlessly searched on the preceding Saturday, almost the first object upon which my eye fell was the ball partially concealed by a stone. Child as I was, my joy was very great. At noon I ran hastily home to inform my mother, knowing that she would rejoice with me over my recovered treasure. After sympathizing with me in my childish happiness, she remarked that Sir Matthew Hale had said that he never passed the Sabbath well without being prospered the succeeding week.

"You remember, my son," she continued, "that you were a good boy yesterday. This shows you, that if you would be happy and prosperous, you must remember the Sabbath day, and keep it holy."

Whether this remark be without exception true, it is not in place now to inquire. That it generally is true, but few will doubt. But the remark in the connection in which it was made, produced an impression upon my mind which will never be effaced. All the other events of that early period have long since perished from my memory; but this remains fresh and prominent. Often has it led me to the scrupulous observance of the Sabbath—even to the present day I can distinctly perceive its influence.

The connection in my mind between God's blessing and the observance of the Sabbath is so intimate that scarcely does a Sabbath morning arrive in which it is not involuntarily suggested. Probably every reader can recall to mind some similar occurrence which has fixed an indelible impression upon his mind. If a mother will be ever vigilant to improve such opportunities, she will make her instructions far more effective than they otherwise would be, and altogether avoid the danger of making religion a wearisome and unpleasant topic.

There is hardly any person so reckless of eternity, so opposed to piety, who will not at times listen to religious conversation. A Christian gentleman was once a passenger on board a vessel where his ears were frequently pained by the profane language of a rude and boisterous cabin-boy. He resolved to watch for some opportunity to converse with him. One evening the gentleman was lying, wrapped in his cloak, upon the quarter-deck, with a coil of ropes for his pillow, enjoying the beauties of ocean scenery. A gentle breeze was swelling the sails and bearing the ship rapidly over the undulating waters. The waves were glittering with their phosphorescent fires, and reflected from innumerable points the rays of the moon.

Not a cloud obscured the thousands of lights which were hung out in "nature's grand rotunda." The cabin-boy happened to be employed in adjusting some ropes near the place where the gentleman was reclining in the rich enjoyment of his wandering thoughts. A few words of conversation first passed between them, upon some ordinary topic. The attention of the boy was then, by an easy transition, directed to the stars.

He manifested increasing interest, as some simple but striking remarks were made upon the facts which astronomy has taught us. From this the mind of the boy was led to heaven. He stood gazing upon the stars, as the gentleman spake of the world of glory and the mansions which Christ has gone to prepare.

He listened with subdued feelings and breathless attention, as the.conversation unfolded to him the awful scene of judgment. By this time his mind was prepared for direct allusion to his own sins. He was attentive and respectful, while he was kindly but most earnestly entreated to prepare to meet Christ in judgment. The effect produced upon the mind of this wicked lad was evidently most powerful. Whether it were lasting or not, the gentleman had no opportunity to ascertain. But by taking advantage of the stillness of the evening, and the impressiveness of the scene, the turbulent spirit of that boy was, for the time at least, quelled. Religious instruction was communicated to his willing mind. And probably he will often, while a wanderer upon the ocean, gaze upon the stars in his midnight watches, and think of judgment and of heaven. How often can a mother seize upon some similar occasion, and instruct, while at the same time she most deeply interests and most effectually impresses the mind of her child!

## Avoid Introducing Religious Subjects on Inappropriate Occasions

Avoid introducing religious subjects upon inappropriate occasions. There are times when serious injury is done by urging the claims of religion. Your child is angry. His flushed cheek and violent motions show the sinful irritation of his mind. Shall the mother now converse with him upon the wickedness of these feelings and God's displeasure? No! It is unseasonable. It would be as unavailing as to converse with a madman, or one intoxicated. Punish him for his irritation in some way which will soothe his feelings and lead him to reflection. But wait till these passions have subsided before you attempt to reason with him upon their impropriety, and to lead him to evangelical repentance.

Kneel by his bedside in the silence of his chamber, and in the pensive hour of evening. When his mind is calm, and passion is not triumphing over reason, he will hear you, and may be melted to contrition. When Peter denied his Master, he did it with cursing and swearing. But when his fears had subsided, and the hour of reflection came, with a sad heart he entered the hall of Pilate. Then did a single glance from the Savior pierce his heart, "and he went out and wept bitterly."

A child is highly excited with pleasurable emotions. His attention is so highly engrossed by the immediate object of his enjoyment, that it is almost impossible to draw his thoughts to any other subject. If, under these circumstances, an effort is made to convince him of the uncertainty of human enjoyments, of his own sinfulness, of the need of a Savior, the effort will not only, in all probability, be unavailing, but the subject will be so unwelcome as to excite disgust. There are times when the mind is prepared with gratitude to receive religious instruction. Let such occasions be improved. There are others when the mind is so manifestly engrossed in one all-absorbing subject, that it is in vain to present any other. If you would not connect religion with unpleasant associations, and excite repugnance, do not on such occasions obtrude this subject.

If a gunner should enter a forest and walk along loading and firing at random, he might accidentally get some game, but most assuredly he would frighten away far more than he would secure. If a parent, with blind and unthinking zeal, is incessantly throwing out random remarks, she may by chance produce the desired effect. She will, however, more frequently excite opposition, and confirm rebellion, than lead to penitence and prayer.

Guard against long and tedious conversations on religious subjects. The mind of a child cannot be fixed for any great length of time upon one subject without exhaustion. Every word that is uttered, after there are manifestations of weariness, will do more harm than good. If a mother will exercise her own judgment, and gather wisdom from her own observation, she will soon acquire that facility in adapting her instructions to the occasion which will have the best tendency to improve her child. No rules can supersede the necessity of personal watchfulness and reflection.

# 8

# Religious Instruction (Continued)

## Make the Bible Your Textbook

Make the Bible your text book in the religious instructions of your children. Few moderns have attained greater celebrity than Lamartine. As a poet, a statesman, an orator, he has filled the world with his renown. When a child, his mother was his intellectual guide, and the Bible the book from which she taught him. She inspired him with all that is noble in his nature, arousing his affections, enkindling his mind, guiding his thoughts, forming his tastes.

The Bible was her text book. Under its guidance, she led her noble and ardent boy through the groves and by the crystal streams of Eden. With her he gathered the fruit, and plucked the flowers, or listened to the songs, of Paradise. He saw depictured before him Adam and Eve in their innocence and bliss, and in their condition and history he saw and felt the beauty of holiness.

The Fall came with its gloom and withering curse. In the howling tempest, the desolation of the garden of Eden, and the weary wanderings of our first parents when ejected from their early home, he saw the hatefulness of sin. The Deluge then succeeds with its blackness of darkness, and its surging billows overwhelming a struggling world. The heart of the child throbs in the conception of the awful scene as a mother's lips tell the tale. His mind is expanded, and his whole spirit elevated by the terrific idea. Babel rises before his eye.

The story of Joseph and his adventurous life inspires him with lofty desires. Daniel, the heroic and the noble, awakens in his bosom the firm resolve that he also will be a Christian hero, daring to do and to suffer, though the famished lion roar, and the heated furnace glow. The Savior, in all the perfection of moral loveliness, and in all the grandeur of moral sublimity, becomes the object of his youthful love and admiration. His bosom glows with lofty emotions at the recital of the eventful lives of the Apostles. His character is thus formed upon the model of the sacred heroes. The mother, with the Bible, aided by God's blessing, has ennobled and saved the boy.

At length, she dies and molders to the dust. Life, with its tempests, rolls over her son. Temptations crowd around his path in sanguine youth and in vigorous manhood. But there is a guardian angel ever hovering over him. That gentle and familiar voice which taught him in infancy never dies upon his ear. That sweet maternal smile never fades from his eye. After long years of toil and conflict have passed away, Lamartine resolves to visit in person the land to which the instructions of his mother had so often led his youthful mind.

The evening twilight is just settling down over the hills of Judea as he catches the first dim glimpse of their outline. The fresh breeze urges the ship over the blue expanse of the Mediterranean, and the moon rises brightly over Carmel and Olivet and Lebanon. His mother first guided his spirit Holy Land. And now his thoughts involuntarily turn to her. "Dear Lord, thank you for the influence of my sweet, precious mother." With a soul swelling with emotion, with eyes swimming in tears, he looks upon the unveiled Heavens above him and exclaims, "Father in heaven, may my life honor the memory of my dear, dear mother! here am I drawing near to your own loved Jerusalem. I am to weep upon Olivet and upon Calvary. Upon the shores of the river and the lake I am to tread in the footsteps which my merciful Saviour trod. Dear God-Mother is not with me anymore, but I know that you are with me, and that you sympathize in the joy of your child."

Thus does the spiritual sympathy which binds the heart of a child to a mother, survive, and continue to exercise its power, long after that mother has been slumbering in the grave. The Bible is the strongest of all influences in the creation of that sympathy. There is, in its relations, the union of all that is intellectually exciting, and all that is spiritually sacred. Its narratives, its imagery, its precepts, it's thrilling and heroic incidents, all more powerfully move the human heart than any other agency.

We have not sufficient faith in the potency of the Bible. It should be to the parent her manual, her armory, a treasury for her of every blessed influence. The infant mind eagerly listens to the recital of the biography and the history with which its pages are filled. Tell your child the stories of Eden—of the Fall, and of the Deluge—of the cities of the plain, wrapped in fire—of Samuel, and Joseph, and Moses, and David, and Ruth, and Daniel. Read to them these narratives in the beautiful simplicity with which the pen of inspiration has recorded them, and you will awaken a strong and abiding interest in his mind; you will fortify him against the wiles of infidelity, with arguments more potent than all the demonstrations of philosophy; and you will ally your name, a mother's name, with the Bible, with angels, with heaven, with God.

The mother must not surrender the instruction of her children in the narratives and truths of the Bible, to others—to the Sabbath-school teacher or her pastor. Grateful as she may be for the Sabbath-school, and the church, and all the benign influences which they exert, it is her privilege, her peculiar privilege, her inestimable privilege—a privilege of which no one may deprive her, to take her child by the hand herself and lead him to the Savior.

She must reveal to the tender and awakened spirit, death and its struggles, the grave and its corruption—the archangel's trumpet, the morning of the resurrection, the sublimity and the terror of the final judgment. A mother's loving voice must guide the mind to the garden of God on high—its blest mansions, it's still waters, its green pastures, its fullness of never-fading joy. A mother's gentle tones must reveal all that is awful in the retribution of a righteous God, and the remorse and the despair, which, like an undying worm and a quenchless flame, must consume the sinner's heart. In doing this, the Bible should ever be the parent's storehouse of religious influence. It is the mighty power of God.

## Aim at Interesting Children in Moral Truths and Sentiments

In teaching children from the Scriptures, aim at interesting them in the moral truths and sentiments which the narratives convey. In fact, upon a proper use of the sacred volume, a great deal depends in respect to the success which is to be obtained through its instrumentality. There are some parts of it which children can at a very early age understand and appreciate. Others, from their style or subject, will act efficiently on mature minds alone.

From the former, which ought to be early read and explained, an immediate and most important religious influence can at once be exerted. Selections from the latter should be fixed in the memory, to exert an influence in future years. For the former of these purposes the narrative parts, if judiciously selected, are most appropriate in early years. But great care ought to be taken to select those which may be easily understood, and those in which some moral lesson is obvious and simple. Let it be constantly borne in mind that the object in view in teaching the Bible to a child, is to affect his heart; and it would be well for every mother to pause occasionally, and ask herself, " What moral duty am I endeavoring to inculcate now? What practical effect upon the heart and conduct of my child is this lesson intended to produce?"

To ask a young child such questions as, "Who was the first man?" "Who was the oldest man?" "Who slew Goliath?" may be giving him lessons in pronunciation, but it is not giving him religious instruction. It may teach him to articulate, or it may strengthen his memory—but is doing little or nothing to promote his piety. I would not be understood to condemn such questions. I only wish that parents may understand their true nature. If the real or supposed dexterity of the child in answering them is not made the occasion of showing him off before company—thus cherishing vanity and self-conceit—it may be well thus to exercise the memory; and some facts, which will be useful hereafter, may be fixed in this way. But it must not be considered as religious instruction;—it has not in any degree the nature of religious instruction.

What, then, is the kind of instruction which is to be given from the Bible? I will illustrate the method by supposing a case which may bring the proper principles to view. We will imagine the child to be two or three years old.

"Come," says its mother, "come to me and I will read you a story." It is Sabbath afternoon we will suppose; the mind of the child is not pre-occupied by any other interest.

"Sometimes," continues the mother, "I tell you stories to amuse you. But I am not going to do that now. It is to do you good. Do you understand how it will do you good to hear a story?"

"No, mother."

"Well, you will see. It is the story of Cain and Abel. Do you know anything about it?"

"Yes; Cain killed Abel."

"Do you know why he killed him?" "Because he was wicked."

"No, I mean what did Abel do to make Cain angry with him? Did you ever see anybody angry? Were you ever angry yourself?"

"Yes, mother."

"And I suppose you had some cause for it. Now I will read the account, and see whether you can tell what made Cain angry. 'And Cain brought of the fruit of the ground an offering unto the Lord.' Do you know what the fruit of the ground is?"

"No, mother."

"It means anything which grows out of the ground. Cain was a farmer; he planted seeds and gathered the fruits which grew from them, and he brought some of them to offer them to God. 'And Abel brought of the firstlings of his flock.' Do you know what that means?"

The child hesitates.

"Abel did not cultivate the ground like Cain. He had great flocks of sheep and goats, and he brought some of the best of those to offer to God. So that you see that Cain and Abel did almost exactly the same thing.

"Now, God does not notice merely what we do, but how we feel, while we are doing it. If I should ask you to go and shut that door when you are busy, and if you should go immediately, but feel ill-humored, God would be displeased. He looks at the heart. Do you ever feel illhumored when I wish you to do what you dislike?"

"Yes, sometimes."

"Now, Cain, I suppose, did not feel pleasantly when he brought his offering, and God was dissatisfied with him. But God was pleased with Abel's offering, and accepted it. Should you have thought that Cain would have liked this?"

"No:—did he like it?"

"No, he did not. He was very much displeased; and it is very remarkable that he was displeased, not only against God, but he was angry with his brother, who had not done him the least wrong. That is the way with us all. If you should do wrong, and your sister do right, and I should blame you, and praise her, you would be tempted to feel angry with her, just because she had been so happy as to do her duty. How wicked such a feeling is!

"Cain, however, had that feeling; and little children have it very often. It shows itself in different ways. Cain, being a strong man, rose against his brother in the field and killed him. But young children who are weak and small would only strike each other, or say unkind things to one another. Now God is displeased with us when we have these feelings, whether we show them by unkind words, or by cruel violence. There is a particular verse in the Bible which shows this. Should you like to have me find it?"

"Yes, mother."

"I will find it then. It is in Matt. v. 22, Our Savior says it. It is this, ' Whosoever is angry with his brother without a cause, shall be in danger of the judgment; and whosoever shall say, Thou fool, shall be in danger of hellfire.' This is not the whole of the verse. I will explain the other part some other time."

The reader will perceive at once that the kind of instruction here exemplified, consists in drawing out the moral lesson which the passage is intended to teach, and in giving it direct and practical application to the circumstances and temptations of the child.

The views which are generally entertained of heaven, as described in the Bible, are far more indefinite than they ought to be. This home of the blest is described in the Scriptures with the most magnificent imagery that nature affords. Heaven is spoken of as having a distinct locality, like any place on earth. We hear of the splendor of the golden city, adorned with every beauty with which the hand of Omnipotence can embellish it; of the mansions glittering with architectural magnificence. We are informed of the social enjoyments of that world.

The Christian is introduced to the society of angels; converses with them; unites in their enjoyments; becomes a loved member of their happy community. We are informed of the active delights of heaven. Angel bands fly to and fro, the rejoicing servants of God. They unfold their wings and take their rapid flight where all the glories of the universe allure their curiosity, and where no darkness succeeds the splendor of ceaseless day. The eye gazes full and undazzled upon the brightness of God's throne. The ear is charmed with melody. The body of the Christian is to arise from the grave, incorruptible and immortal. There is the union of soul and body in that happy world. There we meet our Christian friends; recognize them; rejoice in their love. Thus we pass our eternity with songs, and everlasting joy upon our heads, where sorrow and sighing forever flee away.

How vivid and impressive are the views which the pen of inspiration gives of the Christian's future abode! Yet the very common idea entertained of heaven is, that it is a vast aerial expanse, where shadowy and unsubstantial spirits repose in mysterious and indefinable enjoyment. There is, indeed, with many individuals, an impression that it is wrong to associate ideas of joys with which we now are familiar, with that celestial abode. But is it not safe, is it not a duty, to be guided in our instructions by the Bible? Admitting that the descriptions of the Bible are figurative, as they of necessity must be, still these are the figures which God has employed to convey to our minds an idea of the joys of heaven. And God would surely select the most appropriate figures, and those which most nearly resemble the enjoyments to be illustrated.

## Describe Heaven to Our Children

It is our privilege and our duty, therefore, to describe heaven to our children, as God has described it to us. Thus may we give it vividness in their minds. Thus may we excite in their youthful bosoms the most intense desire to enter that happy world. And why has God unfolded its glories but to allure us to holiness and entice us home? Your son has an unusual thirst for knowledge. His curiosity is ever on the alert. He is prying into nature's mysterious movements, and asking questions which the human mind cannot answer.

Tell him that there are no limits to human improvements; that the grave cannot enchain the energies of mind; that time cannot circumscribe its range; that eternity cannot weary its powers; that it will advance in its acquisitions, and soar in its flight, long after suns, and moons, and stars shall have waxed old and decayed. Tell him that in heaven he shall understand all the wonders of God's works, and experience the most exquisite delight, as he looks into and comprehends all the machinery of nature. And then you can tell him of the Savior, who died that he might introduce him to this happy world.

Your daughter has an ear charmed with the melody of sound. Music is to her a source of exquisite enjoyment. Is there no music in heaven? Is there no melody in the "chorus of the skies?" Is there nothing enrapturing to the soul while uniting with angel bands in their hallelujahs? God has thus described heaven to us. Why should we not then animate our children with the same description? You may, in familiar language, carry the thoughts of your daughter away to companies of happy angels, with celestial harps and divine voices rolling their notes of joy through heaven's wide concave. Thus will she have some definite idea of the enjoyments to which she is invited. The joys of heaven will be to her intensely alluring; and she will be led to inquire more earnestly into the way of salvation, and with more fervor to implore God's aid to overcome sin and prepare her for a heavenly home.

Your child has an affectionate disposition, a heart open to receive friendship, and to pour forth its love. Tell him of the love of heaven, of God, of the angels. Tell him of the love which animates the bosoms of those noble spirits who have not a single fault to repel attachment. Tell him of again meeting all his friends who love the Savior, in that world where an unkind word, or an unkind look, or an unkind thought is unknown. And as you dwell upon the proofs of a Savior's love, his heart may be melted.

Is your child passionately fond of nature's scenery? Does he look with a poet's eye upon the ocean, upon the starry canopy, upon the gilded clouds of sunset? There surely is magnificence in the scenery of heaven. There is splendor worth beholding in the visions of angels, the throne of God, the wide-spread universe of countless worlds. What is the ocean but a drop sprinkled from the almighty hand? What is Niagara, to us so magnificent, but a tiny rivulet rippling over its pebbly channel?

Animate your child with the description of those glories of heaven, before which all the sublimity of earth sinks to insignificance. Fear not that this will extinguish in his bosom a taste for nature's beauties. It will, while increasing the enjoyment which he derives from these sources, refine and elevate his mind, and give him ardent desires to be prepared for this world of glory. Fear not that this will strengthen in his heart the principles of selfishness instead of leading him to piety. If God had felt such fears, he never would have presented us the allurements of heaven, or the terrors of hell. Present these joys, that your child may be induced by them to repent of sin, to trust in the Savior, and to consecrate life to his service.

These descriptions are necessarily in some degree figurative, and we must so instruct our children. But we must not neglect the use of these figures, for they convey to the mind the most correct conception that can be attained of the enjoyment of the future world. The fact that God has selected them, proves that no other language can be equally appropriate. They describe, as perfectly as human language can describe, the nature of heaven's enjoyments. But they do not come up to the realty; for eye hath not seen, nor ear heard, nor human heart conceived, the joys which God has prepared for those who love him.

God knows how to adapt instruction to the human mind. We must imitate his example. And we must present heaven to our children as God has presented it to us, crowded with images of delight. The purest and noblest joys that we experience on earth, will be found again in that world, only infinitely elevated and refined. And he must adopt singular principles of interpretation, who does not read in the Bible, that in heaven we shall find splendor of scenery, harmony of music, congeniality of companions, ardor of love, delight of active motion, mansions of glory, and homes of never failing bliss. Let us urge these views upon our children till their hearts are warmed by them. Nothing can have a stronger tendency to convince them of the folly of laying up treasures upon earth. And this will lead them to listen with interest to your instructions in order that they may learn how salvation is to be obtained.

## Carefully Culture Our Own Hearts

Next to the Bible, as a means of religious influence, we must place the careful culture of our own hearts. The parent must strive to be herself, just what she wishes her child to be. She must cherish in her own spirit those virtues and those graces, which she desires to see as the embellishments of the character of her child Our children have more right to expect that we shall be model parents than we have to require that they shall be model children. Their temptations are as severe for them as ours are for us. We are apt to think their burdens light, because upon our mature minds they would press with but little weight. And thus most erroneously we excuse ourselves for defects which we censure severely in them.

Would you have your children look to God sincerely, affectionately, cheerfully, as their Father and their friend—their sympathizer in joy, their comforter in sorrow? Lead them to do this, by your example. Let them see this spirit in you. When you bend over the cradle of a dying child, when disaster comes and sweeps away your means of luxury and even of comforts, when disease takes you from the busy cares of the household and you languish in debility and pain upon your bed—then is the time, in which to show the loveliness and the blessedness of confidence in God. A smile upon your countenance, a glance of confiding affection in your eye, a word of calm submission from your full heart, will then go to the hearts of your observing children, with great and effectual power. Words are air. They fall upon the ear, and are forgotten. But who ever forgets abiding, consistent, unvarying example? What child ever ceases to remember the life, the daily life, of its father and its mother?

The ornaments and graces too, of the natural character as well as the principles of piety, can best be inculcated upon children through the influence of example. Would you have your daughter learn to control her passions, and cultivate a subdued, gentle, and submissive spirit? Would you have her speak soothingly to her little brother, when he is irritated, and bear her own little troubles without fretfulness or complaining? Show her how to do it by your example. When the careless domestic drops the china vase, or spoils the dinner, or breaks the lamp of oil upon the carpet; then is the time, in which to teach your child how to govern herself. This is your hour of conflict. Gain the victory yourself, and your child will gather strength from your success to struggle with her own temptations and sins.

Say not that the annoyances and trials which you have to bear, are too great to be always endured with equanimity. God lays upon his children no intolerable burdens. We need such discipline as these things bring that we may be able to sympathize with our children in their trials. And we surely ought not to be surprised to find that our children get vexed and angry at the disappointments and injuries which befall them, if we lose our own tempers and resent with ruffled feelings and angry words the acts of carelessness on the part of others by which we are annoyed.

Parents should never, especially in the presence of their children, give way to feelings of irritation and anger. Even when a child does wrong, there should be no expression of resentment or vexation in our looks or in our words. We may act firmly on such occasions, and reprove effectually, while yet we maintain throughout, the quiet, gentle, and peaceful spirit by which the conduct of the Christian ought at all times to be characterized.

In fact, the efficiency of parental discipline will depend in a great measure upon the mildness and gentleness of the form it assumes: while at the same time, by assuming such a character, it makes the subject of it gentle and mild.

In the same manner, feelings of benevolent regard for the happiness of others, and all other right moral sentiments of heart, can be best cultivated through the influence of parental example. Would you cherish in your child, a heart to feel for others' woes—a generous spirit, active in the relief of distress?

Take your son or your daughter with you, as you grope through the dark passage-way to the room of sickness and penury. Let him see the scanty furniture, the thin clothing, and the feeble flame dying on the hearth. Let him bear, himself, the basket which conveys comforts to the desolate; and the spirit which glows in your bosom, will warm his also; and the spirit of benevolence which Christ has kindled in your bosom, will diffuse its warmth into his youthful heart.

It is a beautiful arrangement of Providence that requires that the great work of the formation of the character of children should be done in the heart of the parent herself. I am to teach my child to avoid vanity, and pride, and selfishness, by cultivating within myself, with never-tiring assiduity, the spirit of lowliness, of humility, of self-sacrifice. It is thus, more effectually than in any other way, that I am to reach and influence his heart. So I am to curb (the impetuous passions of my child, mainly by gaining the victory over myself, and bringing all my own passions under perfect control. It is thus within myself—it is in my own heart, that I can work most effectually in molding the character of my children; for in promoting their moral progress I must go before them and lead the way.

What fearful questions, then, arise in the mind of every parent? Am I what I wish my child to be? Am I grateful, submissive, cheerful? Have I conquered my passions, been weaned from the world, and am I daily, in my life, presenting an example such as my child may safely imitate? Here lies the great work of parental faithfulness. Here is to be laid the deep foundations of all salutary family discipline. Thus did our Savior plead. Such was the influence he wielded. Persuasive as were his words, infinitely more persuasive was the power of his example.

## Dwell Particularly Upon the Savior

Dwell particularly upon the Savior, in the religious instruction of children. The Scriptures declare that the preaching of Christ crucified is the great instrument which God uses in convincing of sin, and leading the soul to penitence and gratitude. And the history of the church in all ages has shown that the history of a Savior's love and death will awaken contrition and melt the heart, when all other appeals are in vain. Your child will listen, with tearful eye, while you tell of the Savior's elevation in heaven; of his becoming man; of the sufferings and persecution of his life; and of his cruel death upon the cross. And when you tell your child that it was God who thus became manifest in the flesh, and suffered these indignities that he might redeem his sinful creatures from woe, you will convey to the tender mind such an idea of God's kindness, and the ingratitude of sinners, as nothing else can produce.

The philosopher may admire the noble conception of the eternal, incomprehensible, invisible Spirit. But it is God, as manifested in the compassionate, gentle, and suffering Savior, who attracts the sympathies of the heart. A definite idea is introduced to the youthful mind, when you speak of him who took little children in his arms and blessed them. Every Christian can judge, from the effect produced upon his own heart by the recital of a Savior's love, of the tendency it has to awaken in the bosom of a child the deepest emotions of contrition and gratitude. It is very observable, in all the accounts of youthful piety, that the Savior is the prominent object of affection.

Any person will be interested, in turning over the pages of almost any pious child's biography, to witness how strong the impression which a Savior's love produces upon the heart. Even under the most adverse circumstances, the youthful heart has found its way to him. Not a few instances have occurred, in which parents, who have not been accustomed to give prominency to the Savior in their instructions, have been surprised to find that Jesus Christ is the sympathizing friend to whom a child, in sickness and in suffering, has most affectionately clung. God, in Christ, has attractions which nothing else can have.

When little Nathan Dickerman was asked, "What do you love to think about most when you are in pain?"

"The Lord Jesus Christ," he answered.

At another time his biographer records, "Nathan is very-sick to-night. His heart is beating most violently and rapidly, while the pulse can hardly be perceived at the wrist. But he says he is more happy than usual. I asked him why. He replied, "'Because my Savior is near.'

"Being asked which was his favorite hymn; he reflected a moment, and repeated, "One there is above all others Well deserves the name of friend; His is love beyond a brother's, Costly, free, and knows no end. Which of all our friends, to save us, Could or would have shed his blood? But this Savior died to have us Reconciled in him to God."

"The remembrance of what the Savior suffered sustained him in all his sufferings. Redeeming love was the theme of his sweetest meditations.

"One day, someone was mentioning in the room, that his disease was of such a nature that he would probably die suddenly. Nathan heard it, and rising up in the bed, clasped his hands together, and repeated the verse,

"Jesus can make a dying bed Feel soft as downy pillows are,

While on his breast I lean my head, And breathe my soul out sweetly there."

"And after sitting a few moments in silence, he added another:

"Jesus, my God, I know his name,

His name is all my trust;

Nor will he put my soul to shame; Nor let my hope be lost"

"' Isn't that a good hope, mother?' "

We might open to almost any memoir of early piety, in illustration of this principle. And indeed everyone who is familiar with the characteristics of devotional feeling, as they are exemplified in the mind of a child, must have observed the wonderful adaptation of religious truth to our weakness arid frailty.

Let parents, therefore, imitate the apostles, and preach to their children a suffering Savior. Show them God in Christ, reconciling the world to himself. This is the simplicity of the Gospel. Indeed, we can hardly conceive it possible for the affections of a child to cling with ardor to any object, of which it cannot form some definite conception. Tell your child of Christ, who created him; of Christ, who became man, and suffered and died to save him; of Christ, before whose judgment seat he soon must appear; of Christ, whose praises the Christian will sing in heaven, ages without end. Thus is God, if I may so express it, simplified to the comprehension of the child.

The mother who does not often present this Savior, and dwell upon the story of his sufferings and death, has not yet learnt the simplicity and power of the gospel. All other motives are feeble, compared with this. You may search the world of fact and of imagination in vain for any motive calculated to produce so deep an impression upon the mind. And everything in this astonishing occurrence has a tendency to promote humility, and penitence, and love. I dwell the more earnestly upon this point, for it appears to me of primary importance. It is the all-availing instrument which God has given to subdue the power of sin in the heart.

Pray with your children. It is not only the duty of a mother to pray for her children, but when they are young, to pray with them. Let them hear your fervent supplications that God will make them his friends. Let them see that your desires are intense that they may be preserved from sin, and prepared for heaven. The feelings which animate the bosom of the mother will, by sympathy, in some degree, be transferred to the bosoms of the children. These scenes of devotion will long be remembered. And even if your efforts and your prayers are not answered with the early evidences of your children's piety, these hours of devotion will leave a trace upon the memory never to be effaced. Through all succeeding years they will operate as restraints from plunging into guilty excess, and as monitions of conscience calling loudly to repentance and virtue.

It is reported of a man, eminent for his talents, his elevated situation in life, and his dissipation, that one evening, while sitting at the gaming-table, he was observed to be unusually sad. His associates rallied him upon his serious aspect. He endeavored, by rousing himself, and by sallies of wit, which he had always at command, to turn away their attention, and throw off the transient gloom. Not many moments transpired before he seemed again lost in thought, and dejected, by some mournful contemplations. This exposed him so entirely to the ridicule of his companions, that he could not defend himself. As they poured in upon him their taunts and jeers, he at last remarked, "Well, to tell the truth, I cannot help thinking, every now and then, of the prayers my mother used to offer for me at my bedside when I was a child. Old as I am, I cannot forget the impressions of those early yours."

Here was a man of highly cultivated mind, and of talents of so high an order as to give him influence and eminence, notwithstanding his dissolute life, and yet, neither lapse of years, nor acquisitions of knowledge, nor crowding caret, nor scenes of dissipation, could obliterate the effect which a mother's devotions had left upon -his mind. The still small voice of a mother's prayers rose above the noise of guilty revelry. The pious mother, though dead, still continued to speak in impressive rebuke to her dissolute son. Many facts might be introduced illustrating the importance of this duty. The following is so much to the point, and affords such cheering encouragement, that I cannot refrain from relating it.

A few years since, a gentleman from England brought a letter of introduction to a gentleman in this country. The stranger was of accomplished mind and manners, but in sentiment an infidel. The gentleman to whom he brought letters of introduction; and his lady, were active Christian philanthropists. They invited the stranger to make their house his home, and treated him with every possible attention. Upon the evening of his arrival, just before the usual hour for retiring, the gentleman, knowing the peculiarity of his guest's sentiments, observed to him that the hour had arrived in which they usually attended family prayers; that he should be happy to have him remain and unite with them, or, if he preferred, he could retire. The gentleman intimated that it would give him pleasure to remain. A chapter of the Bible was read, and the family all knelt in prayer, the stranger with the rest.

In a few days the stranger left this hospitable dwelling, and embarked on board a ship for a foreign land. In the course of three or four years, however, the providence of God again led that stranger to the same dwelling. But O, how changed! He came the happy Christian, the humble man of piety and prayer. In the course of the evening's conversation he remarked that when he, on the first evening of his previous visit, knelt with them in family prayer, it was the first time for many years that he had bowed the knee to his Maker.

This act brought to his mind such a crowd of recollections, it so vividly reminded him of a parent's prayers which he had heard at home, that it completely absorbed his attention. His emotion was so great that he scarcely heard one syllable of the prayer which was uttered, from its commencement to its close. And God made this the instrument of leading him from the dreary wilds of infidelity to the peace and the joys of piety. His parents, I believe, had long before gone to their rest; but the prayers that they had offered for and with their son, had left an influence which could not die. They might have prayed ever so fervently for him, but if they had not prayed with him, if they had not knelt by his side and caused his listening ear to hear their earnest supplications, their child might have continued through life un-reconciled to his Maker.

There is efficacy in prayer. God hears and answers our requests. But he does this in accordance with the laws which he has established. It is presumption to expect that he will interrupt the harmony of those laws. He acts through them. And we should endeavor to accommodate all our efforts to the known habits and laws of mind; to present those motives which have a tendency to influence. God answered the prayers of these pious parents; but he did it through the instrumentality of the very effort which they were making in asking him to bless their son, though their efforts seemed for a time to lead to no result.

## Teach Your Children to Pray Themselves

Teach your children to pray themselves. It may be very useful to teach a child the Lord's Prayer and other simple forms. And a child may thus really pray—give utterance to his own feelings in the language of another. But this cannot supersede the necessity of teaching him to go himself to thank God for all the nameless enjoyments of the day, and to ask forgiveness for the various faults he may have committed. The minds of children dwell upon particulars. They are not in habits of generalizing.

It requires but little feeling to confess that we are sinners. But to specify individual acts of wickedness demands a much greater exercise of humility. And a general recognition of God's goodness affects the mind very differently from the enumeration of particular mercies. It is therefore important that your child should be taught to review the events of each day at its close. He should be reminded of the mercies received, and the faults committed; and be taught to express gratitude for the one, and implore pardon for the other. The return of a father from a journey has given your children an evening of very unusual enjoyment. When they retire for the night, allude to the happy evening they have passed. Tell them it was God who preserved their father's life, and returned him safely home. And having thus excited real gratitude in their hearts, lead them to express this gratitude in their own simple and artless language.

By thus pointing their attention to prominent facts and individual blessings, they will not only acquire facility in prayer, but be most effectually taught their entire dependence upon God.* Care should also be taken not to overlook the ordinary blessings of life. It is a rainy day. Show God's goodness in sending the rain. Let them see distinctly that their Father in heaven does it that his children may have food to eat. It is night. Show them the consequences which would result if God should never again cause the sun to rise and shine upon them. They haye received some needful clothes. Show them how God makes the wool grow, that they may be warm. Every mother can easily present to them such contemplations, which will enlarge their field of thought, increase their knowledge of God, promote gratitude, and give a facility in prayer which will be to them a permanent and valuable acquisition.

Let it not be said that to impart such instructions as these requires a degree of knowledge and skill which but few parents possess. The chief difficulty to be surmounted is the feeling which so many parents entertain that they have not time. But the mother who feels the importance of this subject as it deserves to be felt, will find time to be faithful with her children, whatever else she may be under the necessity of neglecting. The same course should be pursued in confession of sin. By pointing to these mercies you may easily convince your child of its want of suitable gratitude. Perhaps he has, during the day, been guilty of falsehood, or disobedience, or anger.

Point to the definite case, and lead your child to confess it before God, and ask forgiveness. We will suppose that your son has been irritated, and struck his sister. Before he falls asleep, you remind him of his sin. Show him how wicked it was, and how displeased God must be. Tell him when he is asleep he will die, unless God keeps him alive. Under such instructions, almost every child would desire to ask forgiveness, and probably would offer some such prayer as this: "0 God, I am very wicked. I struck my sister. I am very sorry, and will never do so again. O God, forgive me, for Jesus Christ's sake."

This would be prayer, if offered from the heart; and if, after it had been offered, the mother should kneel by the bedside, and confess the sin of her child, and pray that God would forgive him, in all probability the intended effect of prayer would be accomplished. The offender would be penitent, and the sin forgiven. For these reasons, it is a most obvious duty to teach children to express their own feelings in their own language. And the careful mother may make this exercise one of the most efficient instruments in teaching her child obedience here, and in training it up for holiness and happiness hereafter.

Parents are apt to smile at the childish expressions which children make use of in prayer, and sometimes fear that their language is irreverent. But God looks simply at the sincerity of the petition, at its importance in the mind of the petitioner. A little child of two and a half years prayed, "Lord, help me to laugh and not to cry when mother washes me in the morning." And does not God look with as kind a regard upon the humble request of this little child, as he does upon the fervent petitions of the man who implores support under some painful operation, or strength to overcome an irritable spirit? Such a request, coming spontaneously from the heart of a child, is genuine prayer, and it shows a state of feeling which ought at all times to be cherished.

## Expect That Your Child Will Become a Christian

Expect that your child will become a Christian. That heart which is susceptible of sorrow and love, is capable of evangelical repentance and love to God. No one can doubt but that, at a very early period in life, a child has all the powers which are employed in the exercise of true religion. Neither can there be any doubt that at that early period the mind is more susceptible of impression, the hold of the world is more feeble, and the current of affection may be more easily turned to God. And facts do hold forth most abundant encouragement. How many little memoirs have recently been issued from the press, which have told the affecting tale of youthful piety! Children of five or six years of age have given the most gratifying evidence of attachment to the Savior.

They have endured pain, and met death, sustained by the consolations of religion. Such facts have been too numerous and too decisive to allow unbelief to be longer excusable. And yet it is to be feared that many parents do not feel their immediate responsibility. They still cherish the impression that their children must attain maturity before they can be decidedly penitent for sin, and the friends of God. But the mother who entertains such feelings as these, is guilty of the most cruel injustice to her child. It is almost impossible that she should be vigilant and faithful in her efforts, unless she expects success. Every mother ought to engage in the duties of religious instruction, with the confident expectation that God will accompany her exertions with his blessing. She ought even to feel that, if her child does not give early evidence of piety, much of the responsibility rests with her.

The Christian experience of the child will undoubtedly differ from that of the man who has passed many years in sin, whose habits are firmly fixed, and whose affections have long been flowing in the channel of worldliness. With such a person the struggle of turning to holiness will often be great, and the sense of sin distressingly intense. But the period of your child's conversion may be at so early a stage of its existence as to leave no trace by which the time of the change can be remembered. The struggle will be comparatively feeble, and penitence will be manifested by the tearful eye and the sad heart, and not always by that deep agony of spirit which not infrequently marks the change of those who have grown old in sin. Much injury is often done by laying stress upon the time when one becomes a Christian. Past feelings are at best but an uncertain test of Christian character.

The great object of inquiry should be as to present feelings and conduct. Is the life now in accordance with the requirements of the gospel? Is the heart now affected with humility, and patience, and gratitude? Is the resolution now strong to live for God? If the sun is shining warmly upon us, it is of but little consequence at what moment it arose. There are many Christians who cannot recollect the time when they became subjects of the new birth. Be not, therefore, anxious upon this point. Indeed, by directing the attention of your child to any particular time when it became a Christian, there is danger of leading the mind to rely upon the supposed experience of that moment, rather than upon continued penitence and devotion. And therefore let every mother do all in her power to awaken in the bosoms of her children emotions of sorrow for sin, and reliance upon Christ. And when she finds these feelings in the heart, and controlling the life, let her thank God, and take courage.

She must watch with maternal solicitude, that temptation be avoided, and that the feeble flame burn brighter and brighter. Christ has entrusted this beloved object to your guardianship. Why should not a mother confidently expect this result to follow her efforts? Has not God encouraged her thus to hope, by promising to aid with his blessing? Has he not encouraged, by again and again crowning such efforts with success? Away then with unbelief. To doubt is to distrust the promise of God. Instruct your child, and pray for your child, and look for an immediate blessing. Thus, in all probability, will your heart be made glad by the fruits of early piety at your fireside; grateful children will honor you through life, and the joys of heaven will be magnified by meeting your loved ones there.

## Do Not Speak to Others of the Piety of Your Child

Do not speak to others of the piety of your child. Great injury is thus often done. A child becomes deeply interested in the subject of religion, and his friends are encouraged to hope that he has really become a Christian. They speak of it to others. It is soon publicly known. He receives much attention; is caressed and flattered. Thus is this little child thrown at once into the very hottest furnace of temptation. We might refer to many painful illustrations of this truth in the memoirs of early piety.

Says the biographer of little Nathan Dickerman, "His feelings were often wounded by the injudicious conversation which was frequently held in his presence.

"Kind friends indulged in perhaps what were well-meant, but sadly ill-judged remarks in his presence. And it is most deeply to be regretted that parents and friends so often, inconsiderately no doubt, speak before children in praise of their persons, in a manner that inevitably fosters vanity, which injures their usefulness and happiness as long as they live.

"Nathan's ear was often greeted with, Beautiful boy! Remarkable boy! What a fine countenance! Certainly the most wonderful case I ever heard of! The half had not been told me."

It is remarkable that, while exposed to such temptations, real humility could have been preserved. And though the grace of God sustained this lovely child, but few would have escaped uninjured.

How often is even the Christian minister sensibly affected by flattery! And can a child safely receive such marked attentions? An honest development of facts, upon this subject, would be exceedingly painful. Humility is one of the cardinal virtues of Christianity. The moment an impression is conveyed to the mind that there is something remarkable and meritorious in penitence for sin, and love for God, the heart is elated with pride. And then things are said, and actions performed, to attract attention. Prayers are offered, and feelings of piety expressed, from the love of ostentation; and the child is " spoiled."

Preserve your child from these temptations, by giving no publicity to his feelings. Carefully cherish at home the flame which is kindled in his bosom. Under your protection, let him acquire strength of principle and stability of character. Gradually introduce him to the more public duties of the Christian life. Teach him humility. Preserve his childlike spirit. In this manner you may lead him along to be a humble, and, at the same time, an active and ardent follower of Christ.

# 9

# Fruits of Piety

NOTHING will conduce more effectually to a mother's success in the work of training up her children to be consistent and useful Christians, than right ideas of the true fruits of piety. We must know what fruits the true spirit of piety will produce, for our own sakes, and also for our children. We must know what points we are ourselves to aim at attaining, in cultivating the Christian character, and also in what direction we are to lead our children. I propose in this chapter to consider what the true fruits of piety, as developed in a Christian family, properly are,

## A Devotional Spirit

A spirit of habitual and sincere devotion is so directly implied in the very idea of piety, that it seems scarcely proper to enumerate it as one of the fruits of piety. And yet the importance of direct and constant efforts to cultivate such a spirit, is often overlooked. By a devotional spirit is meant a spirit of sincere and fervent prayer, and a disposition to associate the thoughts of God and his providence with all the occurrences and events of life. Cherish now this spirit in yourselves and inculcate it upon your children. Teach them, for example, that when their father, or you yourself, assemble them for morning or evening prayer, it is not a mere form, or a duty that they are to witness merely, but to take no part in. Teach them, on the other hand, that they have themselves an active and important duty to perform at these seasons.

"When your father reads the passage of scripture," you can say to them, " you must not be inattentive, but must fix your thoughts upon what he reads, and endeavor to understand its meaning, and to apply the instructions to your own case. And as he addresses God in prayer, you should silently repeat after him all the words of his petition, trying to make them your own. And thus you should make the season of family prayer, a season in which you not merely listen to your father's prayer, but engage in devotion yourselves."

It will not be sufficient to inculcate such a lesson as this upon your children by precept alone; you must lead them to such duties by your example. They must see the evidence of a sincere spirit of devotion in you. To this end you must be diligent in secret prayer, confessing your own sins, and imploring God's assistance to enable you to resist the peculiar temptations to which you are exposed. Social prayer is a great source of spiritual improvement and enjoyment. But it can never take the place of secret prayer. There are sins and temptations to which we all are exposed, which we cannot confess in the presence of anyone but God alone. In our secret prayers, therefore, we should be particular, mentioning by name our secret sins, and our constitutional imperfections

Teach your children these truths. "At the close of the day," you may say to them "when you retire to your chamber for the repose of the night, and before you close your eyes in sleep, retrace, with your thoughts, the scenes of the day. Recall to mind all the duties that you have faithfully performed, and also all the duties that you have neglected, and the temptations to which you have yielded. Among your sins of omission, you see, perhaps, that you did not improve your time in school as well as you ought to have done. Your mother found it necessary to censure you for leaving your clothes in your room in disorder.

You also remember that you felt irritated at some little annoyance from your sister, and though you had sufficient self-restraint to refrain from speaking angrily to her, your feelings were for some time so ruffled as to make you quite unhappy. Reflect upon these faults till you feel how sinful they were in God's sight. You must then confess all these and other similar sins to God, and ask his forgiveness for them." It is thus that you must watch over your own spirit, and teach your children to watch over theirs day after day, and year after year, that you and they may grow in grace. It is only by this spirit of particular and secret prayer, that anyone can make any rapid or sure attainments in the divine life. Nothing can be a substitute for faithful prayer. The moment that you begin to neglect it your heart begins to grow cold, and you become the victim of spiritual desertion. But if you are faithful in devotion, your path through life will be " as the shining light that shineth more and more unto the perfect day." You will soon, in this way, gain such a conquest over all sinful passions, that serenity and peace will be the habitual state of your mind.

## Cheerfulness

A cheerful spirit is so specially enjoined in the Scriptures that it may almost be considered a sin to be melancholy. It is a duty to be happy. Gloom and despondency are not only the consequences of sin, but they are sinful states of the mind. They prove ingratitude, and want of submission to the government of God. I will not say that there may not be particular seasons in life, in the history of individuals, in which they must unavoidably be borne down with sorrow. Now and then, there comes upon an individual an awful calamity, and the strongest mind and the strongest faith are prostrated by it. But, even in these cases, it is by no means certain that it is not the duty of the Christian, to feel such perfect confidence in the wisdom and the benevolence of God's government, as to illustrate the truth of the promise, " Thou wilt keep him in perfect peace, whose mind is stayed on thee."

There can, however, be no question but that it is our duty under all ordinary circumstances, to have a mind serene and peaceful. And while admitting that there may be a great difference, in this respect, in the natural disposition of children, nothing is more certain than that we can cultivate, in them as well as in ourselves, the habit of looking upon the bright side of every object, and, by this cultivation, with more or less difficulty, a spirit of almost uninterrupted tranquility and happiness may be acquired. Young persons, and indeed many older persons, are apt to imagine that, if they are unhappy, it is their misfortune; but the truth is, in general, it is not their misfortune, but their sin. They indulge themselves year after year in those feelings which they know to be wrong, and which gnaw at the heart like a viper biting there.

Suppose when you awake in the morning, before offering your morning prayer, you think of all the blessings with which you are surrounded. You reflect how many persons, during the past night, have been tossed upon beds of pain. "How many have died," you say, "and find themselves facing eternity, unprepared for its awful scenes! My Heavenly Father has kept me alive, and another day is now given me in which to prepare for Heaven. The Lord has provided me with all necessary clothes to wear, and food to eat.

I have kind friends around me; opportunities for doing good opened before me; and if I am faithful in duty this day, how happily may its hours glide along! And above all—blissful thought—if the Lord should see fit to take me from the world to-day, I cannot doubt that he has, for my blessed Savior's sake, forgiven my sins, and that he will take me to Heaven. Every day is carrying me nearer to eternal holiness and happiness. O, how much occasion have I for a heart overflowing with gratitude! I shall indeed be inexcusably ungrateful to my heavenly Father if, when crowned with all these blessings, I have a sad and murmuring heart.

"Heavenly Father," you say, in meditative prayer, " help me this day to manifest my gratitude to thee by happy love. May I so love thee, and serve thee, and have such confidence in thy goodness, and so subdue all those passions which are sinful, and consequently disturb one's peace, and so perform all my duties that I may have a tranquil heart all the day long."

In your morning prayer, you pray for a cheerful spirit, as one of your most important duties and blessings. You then go fortified by prayer from your chamber to the family below, with a placid countenance, and a still more placid heart. If any domestic annoyances arise, you are thus prepared to triumph over them. And there is a mysterious influence by which the serenity and good-nature of one heart are transmitted to all surrounding hearts. As you speak in kind and pleasant tones to the family; as you are continually active in making peace and in keeping peace; in preventing, as far as possible, all occasions of annoyance; and in sacrificing, with alacrity, your own ease and your own rights to make all things go smoothly, —you maintain an unruffled state of mind, which most richly compensates you for every act of self-denial. The reward comes with the duty.

It is surprising what an influence one really warm-hearted, cheerful, disinterested person may thus have upon a whole family. I once heard it said of a certain child, "There can be no sorrow where she is. She has the faculty of making everything go pleasantly, and everyone feel happy." This should be the character of every Christian child; and how much more effectual, in disseminating an atmosphere of enjoyment, may be the efforts of a Christian mother. If any mother will set out, perseveringly and prayerfully, in this course of life, resisting every emotion of discontent, cultivating, day after day and hour after hour, a cheerful and happy spirit, contending against every wrong feeling, and cherishing everything that is lovely and of good report, with an effort, never intermitted, to keep a smile upon her countenance and peace in her heart—she will soon gain such control over herself, and get into such a habit of being happy, that hardly anything can interrupt her joy. If she is sick, she will be happy. If well, happy. She will be happy at home or abroad, at work or at rest, alone or in company. When young she will be happy, and when old she will be happy. And when a dying hour comes, and she looks forward to a home in heaven, while others weep, she will rejoice. ,

"Rejoice evermore," says the apostle Paul. This is a divine command; but is one that we cannot obey without making direct efforts to cultivate the spirit that it enjoins. The mother must then carefully and prayerfully cultivate this spirit of joy. A depressed and gloomy spirit she must resist. It is the spirit of Satan, not of God. It is the element of the world of woe, not of the home of the angel. It is said of the celebrated Wilberforce, that he so carefully, in the early part of his life, watched over his own heart, carefully subduing all emotions of vanity, ambition, selfishness, and irritability, that in the latter part of his life he seemed to have risen above temptation. In respect to those sins which so much disturb the peace of ordinary minds, the struggle with him seemed to be almost over, and the victory complete. The closing years of his life were like the calm and golden glory of a summer's evening.

Not a cloud obscured the horizon of his joys. He was just as happy as the days were long. His children and his grandchildren clustered around him, feeling that his presence dispelled almost every sorrow. His favorite passage of Scripture was, " Be careful for nothing, but in everything, by prayer and supplication, with thanksgiving, let your requests be made known unto God; and the peace of God, which passeth all understanding, shall keep your hearts and minds through Jesus Christ." Now, I cannot doubt that it is in the power of almost every person, by the same culture, to attain the same rich and heavenly joy.

Many persons are unhappy who are surrounded with almost every earthly blessing; and many are very happy, who are deprived of almost every earthly good. Our happiness depends far more upon the state of our hearts than upon anything else. Cultivate, then, a right state of heart, and you will almost surely have a happy life. And do not think that you have any right to be unhappy. If you pass an unhappy day, in gloom and depression, you should repent of it, and ask God's forgiveness, and seek his aid that you may sin so no more. Such a day must be a misspent day. Your gloom must have dishonored the religion you profess. It must have marred the happiness of your friends, your husband, your children, and of all your domestic circle. And it must not only have prevented the possibility of any vigorous efforts in doing good, but the influence of your gloomy example must have repelled others from religion.

Therefore make it a daily duty to be cheerful. Pray that you may be cheerful; meditate upon your blessings; look upon the bright side of everything; and carefully study your own heart, that you may ascertain what those feelings are which disturb the tranquility of your mind, and should therefore be checked, and what those emotions are which are satisfying and pleasurable, and should therefore be cultivated. You probably have no idea how much your usefulness and happiness depend upon the careful cultivation of a cheerful spirit.

## Kindness

The spirit of religion is the spirit of self-sacrifice, of giving up our own convenience, and relinquishing our own rights, that we may promote the happiness of others. We are thus to endeavor, not only to secure the happiness of those we love, but also to promote the happiness of those who are unkind to us, whose characters and manners are disagreeable. We are instructed in the Bible, that we must in this respect imitate God, "who maketh his sun to rise on the evil and on the good, and sendeth rain on the just and on the unjust."

Now we must diligently practice this sentiment ourselves, and diligently inculcate it upon our children. Teach them that it is by no means enough, that we love them that love us; that we are kind to those who are kind to us. Our kindness must be a state of the heart, an established principle of universal application. Wherever we can confer a favor, we must do it gladly, whether they who receive it are deserving or undeserving, and we must thank God for the opportunity of thus doing good.

We must remember that an act of kindness however small, if it proceeds from sincere goodwill, is pleasing to God. We must teach this truth to our children. A little child, for example, is seated at a corner of the fireplace, on a cold winter morning. It is a snug corner—the pleasantest seat in the room. With an entertaining book in her hand she is enjoying her pleasant position. Her brother comes in from the cold. At once, perhaps, the thought arises in her mind, "I got this seat first, and have a right to it. It is so comfortable that I cannot think of leaving it." This is the selfish spirit of earth and sin. But she repels this thought. The spirit of Christianity and heaven springs up in her heart, and, immediately rising from her seat, she affectionately says, "Here brother, you look very cold. Take this warm seat. I am quite warm, and will move a little further from the fire."

Now, God looks down upon that act, and is pleased with it. It is acting like God. Angels look down and love such a spirit, and say, "That is the spirit of heaven; there is a child whom we should wish to have associated with us here."

This spirit you should manifest at all times, and on all occasions, and thus set the example of it to your children. Teach them to be ever ready to do all in their power to make others happy. When with their brothers and sisters, or with their associates at school, they must be ever ready in all things to relinquish their own plans to gratify others. A plate of apples is brought into the room. One is larger and fairer than the rest.

Teach them not to choose that one for themselves, but to select it kindly though unostentatiously, for their brother, or their sister, or the friend who has come to visit them—some play is proposed. Teach them to relinquish their own preference, for the choice of others. So, in everything in which it is not wrong to yield, teach them to give up their own wishes, that they may gratify others.

We must be careful, however, that this amiable and yielding disposition does not degenerate into indecision and fickle-mindedness. We are never to yield in the least degree where it is wrong to do so. Whatever we think to be our duty, that we must mildly and kindly, but firmly resolve to do, at all hazards. We must not say, "It is a little sin, and I will indulge in it to gratify others." Remember that the time is near when we must appear before God's bar; and he will not deem it an excuse for displeasing him, that we did it to please our friends or associates. These temptations we must resist; and God exposes us to them that by resistance we may strengthen in our hearts the principle of obedience to him.

A person may have the most amiable disposition in the world—the kindest and the most gentle—and yet possess such a degree of decision of character as to be willing to encounter any opposition and any obloquy rather than do the least wrong. This was the character of our Savior. He was willing to leave heaven, and all the joys of heaven, and to suffer and die upon the cross, that he might do us good. All this he could do for those who did not love him; who were his enemies, and who, with hatred and insult, nailed him to the cross. Such fearful sacrifices as these our Savior could make to promote the happiness of others. And yet there never was any other person in the world, who had so much decision of character as he. No earthly motive could induce him to do anything in the least degree wrong.

We must all possess the spirit of Christ, if we would be his disciples. We must imitate him in his self-denying kindness; in his forgetfulness of his own comfort, that he might promote the happiness of others; and also in his conscientious discharge of duty at all hazards. To cultivate this disposition, is one important part of the Christian conflict.

## Politeness

Some persons may be surprised in finding politeness mentioned as one of the fruits and evidences of piety. You have, perhaps, ever been accustomed to regard politeness as one of those fashionable graces which belong rather to the gay and thoughtless, than to the serious and devotional. But the truth is that politeness is one of the most important of Christian virtues. "Be courteous," is one of the injunctions of the Bible. Indeed, the Bible contains the most perfect rules of politeness known in the world; and it enforces the observance of those rules, as of infinite importance.

The most perfect definition of politeness that I have ever seen, is "real kindness kindly expressed." Politeness does not consist in flourishing manners and airs, artificially acquired. It is the natural expression of amiable feeling. If we carefully cherish the feelings to which I have alluded under the head of kindness, and, with real and unostentatious benevolence, treat all with whom we associate according to those principles, we shall be truly polite. Our manners will be pleasing to all persons. And persons who have not these feelings, and wish to appear polite, will attain only to the empty and lifeless form. Indeed, it is hard to conceive how one can be a Christian, who is not polite. The Christian character is certainly very defective, where this grace is wanting; for it implies the absence of the most lovely traits of the mind and of the heart.

A writer in one of the apocryphal books says, "A gracious word is better than a gift;" and it is indeed true, that some persons will confer a favor in so repulsive a way that it gives you pain rather than pleasure to receive it. Our real kindness must be kindly expressed. If it be not so, we shall often give more pain than pleasure by that which we intended as kindness.

Let the mother then teach her children, both by precept and example to be always polite Let her feel real kindness for all, and express the kindness that she feels in a kind manner. Let her inculcate these principles upon her children. Show them plainly that both points are essential. It is not enough that there should be a substantial feeling of kindness in the heart; it must be kindly expressed. On the other hand it is not enough that there should be kind expression in words or acts;—there must be kind feeling in the heart.

This distinction may be made very clear to the youngest child by the following example. I was once riding with a clergyman, when we met a poor, lame man walking along the road. The clergyman thought it would be a deed of kindness to help him on his way, and, stopping his horse, said, " Here,'you lame man, get in here!" The poor man was glad of a ride, and got in. The clergyman took no further notice of him, but employed his mind with his own thoughts.

Occasionally the poor man would make some remark; but no attention was paid to what he said, unless it was necessary to answer him, and then the reply was a short yes or no. At length we arrived at the place where the man wished to get out. As he left the carriage, he very warmly thanked the clergyman for his kindness in giving him the ride. Not a word, however, was said in reply to his thanks; but the clergyman merely drove on. Now, the unkind manner in which this favor was conferred, undoubtedly gave far more pain to the poor man than the ride gave him pleasure. It was, indeed, conferring a favor in an extremely unfeeling and unchristian way. The clergyman was exceedingly impolite.

Suppose now that he had added to the substantial favor which he intended to confer the charm of kindness of manner in conferring it. He would have said, "Friend, I have a spare seat in the carriage here—will you not get in and ride a little way?" He would then have cheerfully and socially conversed with the man, and manifested some interest in his history. And when the man left the carriage, and thanked him for the ride, he would have replied, " You are very welcome, sir. I am very happy to have had it in my power to assist you. Good evening, sir." This manner of conferring the favor would have cheered and gratified the lame man, and he would have gone to his home with happy feelings.

It is surprising what a vast amount of happiness may be conferred in a long life, by a kind manner of doing kind things. It is by a careful attention to these little things, as some consider them, that we are to make those happy who are around us. As our whole life is made up of such little things as moments, so is the happiness or the unhappiness of life dependent upon the pains or pleasures with which these swiftlyflying moments may be filled. And it is invariably true, that, that person is the happiest, who does the most to promote the happiness of others.

A selfish man is always an unhappy man. And a selfish child is always an unhappy child: as she sits alone in her corner, eating her apple, which she refuses to share with brother or sister; as she eagerly takes the most comfortable chair in the room; as she grasps the new book, resolved to have the pleasure of reading it first, —she is, and must be, unhappy. Conscience within her is disquieted, and her countenance shows in its un-amiable expression what an uncomfortable heart she has. And just so it is with those, who have passed the period of childhood. The man or woman who has grown up with a selfish spirit, is friendless and joyless. Such persons are often to be seen. They live as it were alone in the world. They love no one, and no one loves them.

And, after a heartless life, they die, and no one laments them.

Let children be trained up then to cultivate a courteous spirit, to speak in kind tones of voice, to use a gentle and pleasant way of doing kind things, and it will promote their happiness every day that they live. It will tend to make all around them happy. Others will imitate their example, and imbibe their spirit. The spirit of politeness will vastly increase our influence too in turning others to the Savior. It will confer honor upon the religion of Christ; for the world judges of Christianity, not so much by the instructions of the Savior, as by the lives of its professors.

There is nothing in this world worth having which can be attained without effort. If you would possess the grace of Christian politeness, you must make it a part of your Christian duty and a subject of prayer. You must resolve in the morning, that you will endeavor through the day kindly to manifest kind feelings. And at night, in self-examination, you must inquire where you have failed in this duty; what opportunities you have enjoyed where you might have contributed to the happiness of others, but in which you have failed to do so. This is the true spirit of heaven. If we are ever to enter heaven, we must have this spirit. And it is here, in this world of sin, that we are to triumph over temptation, and subdue passion, and attain all those lovely traits of character which will make us happy companions for angels, and for the spirits of the just made perfect.

## Fidelity in Little Duties

One great error which nearly all Christians fall into is not being sufficiently punctilious in the performance of what are usually called the little duties of life. We are not sufficiently careful to carry out the principles of Christianity into all our relations as husbands and wives, brothers and sisters, parents and children, neighbors and friends. If you, my reader, whatever your situation in life may be, have sincerely commenced a Christian life, you must make it your daily effort to please God in the performance of every duty, small and great. And it is by your attention to things which many persons deem trivial, that you can most effectually glorify God.

Children particularly are apt to imagine that religious obligation is something far removed above all the ordinary duties of life. They seldom connect the idea of Christian duty with such subjects as order, personal neatness, politeness, and other similar points of what are called sometimes minor morals. But you cannot too assiduously teach them that the principle of piety, if they possess it at all, is to regulate all their conduct, and lead them to do right in little things as well as great things.

In fact, the little things, with children, are the great things; for in their various bearings and relations they involve the highest moral principles. Here is a boy for instance, whose mother has appropriated to his use a couple of drawers, in which he is to keep his clothes; and she has enjoined it upon him to have his clothes neatly folded, and always placed in order. Some day she goes into his room, and, as she opens the drawers, behold, everything is in disorder. In haste to get some article of clothing, the boy has rudely drawn it out, and thrown other things in, unfolded, and now everything is in confusion. The mother is deeply pained that her son should be forming such negligent habits.

It has sent an emotion of real unhappiness to her heart. Her own valuable time is occupied in repairing the effects of his indolence and neglect, and the boy himself is growing up with habits which will extremely diminish his efficiency and usefulness as a man. And now that cannot be called a little sin, which produces such consequences, which makes a mother unhappy, and increases her cares and labors, and which is forming in the child habits which will render him unfit for the future duties of life. As well may a man who sets fire to a city, say that it is a little sin, because he merely kindled a very little fire with a few coals. Teach children then that the eye of God is upon them in everything that they do; and that if they really love him, and wish to please him, they will endeavor to be faithful in all their duties, and in small things as well as great.

The mother must feel this truth herself also and apply it to her own case. Few persons imagine how much ones usefulness and happiness in life depend upon their cultivating a habit of neatness, order, and system, in all that they do. Some ladies will accomplish twice as much all through life as some others, simply because, in their childhood, they acquired the habit of keeping everything in its proper place. Go into their house, and everything appears in order. There is no hurry or bustle. There seems to be no effort in keeping things in order. Other ladies, who have been trained up under different habits, either give up in despair, and indolently sit down in the midst of the confusion which reigns in their house, or they toil and hurry through life, never enjoying any quietness or leisure, and always engaged in putting things in order, but never able to keep them so.

Do not, then, allow children to imagine that it is a little sin to be untidy or negligent. It is one of the most important of their duties to cultivate correct habits in these respects. Teach them that they may thus please God, gratify their parents, adorn religion, and not only prepare for future usefulness, but be useful every day and every hour.

We are very apt to think that if we were in some situation different from that in which we are actually placed, we might do a great deal of good. The young often suppose that if they were out in the world, they might, in various ways, as men and women, serve their Maker; but they imagine that they cannot do much, if anything, to serve God and promote his glory, unless in some important station. But God wishes to have his friends placed in all the different positions in society, that the power of religion may be exhibited in all.

He desires that there should be merchants, and mechanics, and sailors, pious fathers and mothers, and pious children. And the child who is pious, may as acceptably serve God in the situation in which she is placed, as any other persons in the situation in which God has placed them. It is not the station in society that we occupy, to which God looks, but the fidelity with which we discharge the duties of the position in which he has placed us. And the faithful, Christian conduct, even of the smallest child, is as acceptable to him, and perhaps as useful in the accomplishment of his purposes, as the zeal and energy of the most devoted Christian martyr.

Teach these things diligently to your children, and train them up in the habit of neatness and order in all that they do. When they come home from school, let them be taught always themselves to hang up the cap, the bonnet, and the cloak in their proper places; and to put their books away. Teach them to shut the door after them when they pass out or in. Teach them to keep all their picture-books and playthings in order. Show them that it is their duty to attend to all these little things, not as matters of trifling importance, but as Christian duties of the greatest moment, demanding constant watchfulness and care.

These are the ways in which God wishes that the young should evince the power of religion, and glorify him. It is by a conscientious attention to such duties as these, performed because they wish to do that which is pleasing in God's sight, that they are to exhibit the fruits of piety. They must aim, every day, to acquire a character of perfect fidelity in the performance of all these duties; remembering that nothing which tends to the perfection of character is too trivial to call for their efforts and their prayers. The best evidence which either the aged or the young can give of piety, is the conscientious endeavor to be faithful in the discharge of every duty, whatever it may be. Thus we glorify God, and honor the Christian religion, in the best manner.

This is what is meant by the text, "By their fruits shall ye know them." The way in which we are to judge of the piety of all persons, is by their conduct. If a man or woman professes to be a Christian, and yet is unfaithful in the discharge of the ordinary duties of life, the profession is vain. It is so in youth, and it is so in age. The best evidence of piety which anyone can give, is the evidence afforded by the devout Christian fidelity with which he performs all the duties of life, both great and small.

# 10

# Fruits of Piety (Continued)

WE continue in this chapter the enumeration of the several traits of Christian character, which the mother should endeavor to cultivate in herself, and in those under her charge.

## Guard Against a Censorious Spirit

A censorious spirit is a very common sin. And it is one to which females, from their comparatively retired mode of life, are peculiarly exposed. There is hardly any sin against which the Bible warns us in more earnest and impressive terms. The evils and mischief produced by an ungoverned tongue— the ruin it produces in alienating friends, kindling animosities, and disturbing in every way the peace and harmony of society—are topics which have called forth some of the most energetic expressions of the inspired penmen.

"The tongue is a fire, a world of iniquity. So is the tongue among our members that it defileth the whole body, and setteth on fire the course of nature, and is set on fire of hell." "If any man among you seem to be religious, and bridleth not his tongue, this man's religion is vain."

Such are the terms in which the sacred writers speak of the importance of setting a guard upon one's tongue. One single person, of a censorious disposition, will often keep a whole church or neighborhood in turmoil. And every reader of this book has probably often seen great unhappiness produced by the unkind remarks or slanderous reports which others have circulated. Indeed, there are very few persons who have not often had hours of suffering to bear in consequence of unguarded remarks which they have made, and which have, perhaps, been slightly exaggerated, and carried to other ears, by those who are always ready to do mischief. Solomon tells us that if one speaks evil of the king, the "bird of the air shall carry the voice, and that which hath wings shall tell the matter;" by which poetic expressions he would teach us, that there is always someone ready to carry evil tidings.

If you say anything against another person, it is very probable it will be repeated, with exaggerations, to that individual. One will repeat it to another, till the story, gathering in size as it goes, like the balls of snow which boys roll together in the early spring, reaches the ear of the person against whom the remark was made. Then ensues recrimination, unkind treatment, a quarrel. Others are drawn in. And it may be truly said, in the language of the Bible, "Behold how great a matter a little fire kindleth!" The amount of suffering which is caused in this world, simply by evil speaking, is inconceivable. Every school, every church, every neighborhood, is ravaged by it. A very little observation will show you how great is this evil.

Let the mother explain this subject to her children, and caution them against this danger. Lead them to form the resolution that they will never allow themselves to speak against anyone, unless it is clearly their duty to do so. Set them a good example, too, yourselves in this respect. Resolve that you will nip a censorious spirit in the very bud. If you do this, it will save you hours of suffering. If, on the other hand, you allow yourself to speak freely of the faults of others—if you report the various stories you hear—you will be continually in trouble yourself, and will always be involving other persons in difficulty. Resolve that you will not say anything against any absent person—except in cases where it is most undoubtedly your duty to do so—which you would not be willing to have repeated to that person.

There are cases in which it is our duty to speak of the characters of others, and, if their characters are bad, to say so. It may be our duty to warn our children against a vicious and dangerous acquaintance. And when such an occasion clearly arises, we must faithfully perform the duty, however unpleasant it may be. But such cases are comparatively rare, while the fault of evil speaking is one of the most general and inexcusable in the world.

When this habit has once been formed, it is almost impossible to eradicate it. A person who has become a thorough gossip, retailing all the slander which she can collect, is almost beyond the hope of amendment. She will, without the least compunction of conscience, throw suspicions upon the fairest reputation. No character is secure from her backbiting assailment. She becomes blind to her own degraded character, as the village gossip and slanderer. It is surprising how unconscious such a person may be of her odious fault. When she hears anything about evil speaking, she has been so much in the habit of looking at the faults of others, and not at her own, that she does not think of making any self-application, but looks around to see upon whom of her neighbors she can lay the charge.

We have all so many faults of our own to mourn over and to correct, that we should be exceedingly tender of the failings of others And when we see anything in the conduct of our friends or acquaintances, which is wrong or disagreeable, we should try to avoid those things ourselves, and at the same time be very careful and not mention them to others. It is one of the best compliments which can be paid to any lady, to say of her that she was never known to speak ill of others. Resolve, with the grace of God assisting, that this shall be your character, and make every effort to form the same character in your children. Show them that such a habit will multiply their friends; that it will save them many hours of heartache; and that, all their life long, it will greatly add to their usefulness and their enjoyment.

JOHN S. C. ABBOTT

## Teach Your Children to Cultivate Delicacy and Purity of Mind

Teach your children to cultivate, as one of the fruits of piety, scrupulous delicacy and purity of mind. The conscience of children will be a very sensitive guide upon this subject, if it is in a healthy state. Teach them that any conversation which they would be unwilling to engage in, or to repeat in the presence of their mother, they ought to refuse to hear. If their associates at any time commence such conversation, they ought to leave them at all hazards, whether they are offended by it or not. They cannot be too careful respecting the words that they use, or the ideas that they allow to enter their minds.

The delicacy of the mind is very easily impaired, and, when once impaired, the injury is irreparable. Even in the higher walks of life females are often met with who seem to have no sense of propriety. They are always introducing topics of conversation which are revolting to the refined mind, while they themselves have become so obtuse in their feelings, that they appear entirely unconscious of any impropriety. Other ladies have an instinctive modesty and delicacy, which is their brightest ornament. You never hear from them a word, or an allusion, which is not pure and pleasing. The appropriate simplicity of their dress, the softened tones of their voice, the topics of conversation which they introduce, and the gentle expression of countenance, all unite in testifying the spotless purity that reigns in their hearts.

Who can see such a lady, and not esteem and love her? The indelicate of either sex are rebuked by her presence. Even indelicate ladies (if it be not a perversion of language to call one a lady who has an impure mind) are careful, in her presence, to put a guard upon their tongues. "Keep thy heart with all diligence," is one of the cautions which God has given us, and the happiness of every young Christian depends more upon the cultivation of this virtue, than we often imagine. To find, as we go on through life, that our thoughts naturally dwell upon objects which are pure and pleasant, will be one of the richest sources of our earthly enjoyment.

We must necessarily pass many, very many hours in life, with our own thoughts. If our thoughts are such that they give us uneasiness of conscience, and we must be continually struggling against them, we shall have many days of secret, but real sorrow. If, on the other hand, by a careful cultivation of the heart, we have cherished only those thoughts which conscience approves, we shall probably move about, in our daily employments, in tranquil happiness. Explain these principles to your children, and endeavor to lead them to resolve that they will not at school, or anywhere else, engage in conversation, or listen to conversation, which they would not be willing to repeat in the presence of their father and their mother. Let that be with them the test of propriety.

Say to them that if at any time they are in doubt, whether the conversation which they are hearing is proper or not, they must ask themselves, "Am I willing to repeat this to the family, at the tea-table, this evening? If they are not, then they must refuse to hear it. If they cannot turn the conversation, they should leave the company. Teach them to remember that God is always present; that his eye is upon them; that he hears every word that is uttered; that he sees every thought of the heart, and that as they prize his approbation, they must resolve to cherish, with the utmost care, purity of heart.

## The Scrupulous Observance of Truth

A very scrupulous observance of truth should be one of the prominent fruits of piety. To some it may seem that this is almost a needless direction. In fact parents are very slow to be convinced that their children ever tell falsehoods at all. It is an almost invariable rule, that all mothers believe that their children always speak the truth, and it is a rule almost equally invariable, that they are all mistaken. Children generally will say what is false, until they are taught to speak the truth. Sometimes they are thus taught very early; and in such cases the mother, forgetting the infantile falsehoods, says that she never knew her child to tell a lie.

Even in later years it will not do generally to trust to any natural love of truth, to save our children from the sin of falsehood. We must often, in our conversations with them, present this subject to their attention, not in the way of suspicion and fault-finding, but of confidence and good-will. We must explain to them how God regards the sin of falsehood, and cite and explain those passages of Scripture which relate to the subject.

The mother must herself, also, always be honest, and frank, and open, in all her dealings with all her children. Never combine, as many mothers do, with an older child, to deceive a younger one. If you do you must expect that your children will combine together to deceive you. Be honest with them all; and in your dealings with your friends, and neighbors, and acquaintances, be open and sincere. Thus you will lead your children in the right way.

## The Spirit of Forgivenses

The spirit of forgiveness is one of the fruits of piety. The mother must cultivate this spirit herself, and inculcate it upon her children. Teach them that the rule of Christianity is, "Forgive your enemies, and do good to those that despitefully use you and persecute you."

The mother must inculcate this principle, like all the others, by her own example. And next to her own example, the narration of instances of a forgiving spirit will have a greater influence upon children, than any general precepts or exhortations.

I will here, for example, relate such an instance. There was once a rich merchant who had many peculiarities of character which exposed him to ridicule. He was a benevolent man, but he was of such eccentric habits, that a witty writer could easily represent him in a ludicrous light.

Acertain neighbor of his, without any just provocation, published a most insulting pamphlet against him, calling him Billy Button, and holding him up to the laughter of the world, in the most contemptuous and ludicrous attitude in which he could be represented. The publication of such a pamphlet was as gross and cutting an insult as could be inflicted, for there is nothing that the human mind so much recoils from, as derision and scorn. The merchant read the libelous pamphlet, and simply remarked that the writer would probably live to repent of its publication.

Someone informed the writer of the pamphlet of the remark that the merchant had made. He considered it as an angry threat of vengeance, and said that he would take good care to keep out of the merchant's power. But in a few years, in the course of business, the writer of the libel unavoidably became deeply indebted to the merchant, whom he had so wantonly injured, and became a bankrupt. The injured man now had his insulter in his power. For unless he would give up the debt, the writer could never enter into business again, and must always remain a poor man.

By much exertion and after many delays, the unfortunate debtor effected a settlement of his affairs, and obtained a release from his other creditors; but how could he go to the merchant whom he had made the laughing-stock of the public, and who had declared that the libeler would yet live to repent of his publication? It seemed folly to hope that he would forget the wrong, and favor the wrong-doer. But the claims of a suffering wife and children at last compelled him to make the application. Humbled by misery, he presented himself at the counting-room of the injured merchant. The merchant was at his desk alone, and as he turned around and saw his libeler before him, his first words were," Take a seat, sir." The guilty man, trembling with apprehension of the repulse which he so richly deserved, told the piteous tale of his misfortunes, and presented his certificate of release, signed by his other creditors, though he had but a very faint hope of obtaining the signature of one he had so deeply wronged.

The merchant received the certificate, and. as he glanced his eye over it, said, "You wrote a pamphlet against me once, I believe, sir." The wretched man could make no reply. The merchant, saying no more, wrote something upon the certificate, and handed it back to him. The poor debtor in despair received the certificate, expecting to find written upon it something expressive of indignation. But how great was his surprise to see, in fair, round characters, the signature of the merchant, releasing him from his debt! "I make it a rule," said the forgiving man, "never to refuse signing the release of an honest man; and I never heard that you were anything else."

The surprise and joy were too much for the poor creditor, and he burst into tears. "Ah!" said the merchant, "my saying was true. I said that you would live to repent writing that pamphlet. I did not mean it as a threat. I only meant that someday you would know me better, and would repent that you had attempted to injure me. I see that you repent it now." "I do, indeed I do," exclaimed the grateful man. "Well, well, my dear sir," said the merchant, " you know me now. How do you get on? What are you going to do?"

The unfortunate man replied that having obtained a release from his creditors, he had friends who would assist him in getting into business again.

"But how are you to support your family in the mean time?" asked the merchant.

The man's answer was, that having given up every farthing to his creditors, he had been compelled to deprive his family of even common necessaries. "My dear sir," said the merchant, "this will never do—your wife and children must not suffer. Be kind enough to take this to your wife from me," handing him a fifty dollar bill," and keep up a good heart. All will be well with you yet. Set to work with energy, and you may yet see many days of prosperity." The poor man was entirely overcome by his emotions. He could not speak. His feelings forbade all utterance, and burying his face in his handkerchief, he went from the room sobbing like a child.

Stories which afford practical illustrations of any moral principle will generally exert a more powerful influence upon the minds of children than general instructions. The minds of the hearers catch the spirit which the story exemplifies by a sort of moral sympathy.

The mother who is aware of this, will, in her general reading, watch for incidents and passages which she can turn to good account in interesting and instructing her children. These she will read and explain to them at proper times, and enforce the lessons which they are calculated to teach, by additional remarks of her own.

Teach your children thus in every way to cultivate a forgiving spirit. Tell them that this is the spirit of the Bible, the spirit of Christ. No one who has any other spirit can safely offer the prayer, "Forgive us our debts as we forgive our debtors."

## Cultivate a Taste for Pure and Noble Pleasures in Your Children

Cultivate in your children a taste for pure and noble pleasures, instead of a lone of worldly gaiety.

Pure and noble pleasures last. They wear well. They leave no sting behind. The pleasures of worldliness and gaiety do not wear well. They exhaust the powers of body and mind, and all the capacities of enjoyment, prematurely, and leave a sting behind. That is the reason why the Word of God condemns them, and why Christians abstain from them. There is hardly any reproach more frequently cast upon Christians than the charge of bigotry, because they refuse to unite with the world in these scenes of gaiety. They are invited to a ball, to the theater, or to a card-party, and yet no persuasions can induce them to go. "What can be the possible harm," it is said, " in going to a ball?"

We go to a brightly illuminated hall. We have pleasant music to gratify the ear. In graceful measures we beat time to its cadences in the exhilarating dance. After having thus passed a few hours of heartfelt hilarity, we retire unharmed to our homes. Now, what real objection can there be to this amusement," it is asked, "which is not founded on ignorance and superstition?"

This is a very important question, and it deserves a very serious answer. To explain my views upon this subject, let me suppose that you have a son nineteen years of age, a very amiable, correct, and promising young man. He is the hope of the family; attentive to his father and mother, kind to his sisters; all love him. He is a clerk in a store, and is highly respected by his employers. As you have known many amiable young men, in such situations, ruined by dissipation, you feel great solicitude for him. He has so little of selfishness in his nature, and is so willing to sacrifice his own inclinations to oblige others, that, while he thus promises to be one of the best and most useful of men, he is much exposed to be led away by temptation.

Like an affectionate and dutiful son, as he is, he comes to his father some day, and says to him, " Father, there is to be a ball tonight. All my acquaintances are going, and, if you have no objection, I should like to go also."

"Well, my son," says his father, "what time does the ball commence?"

"Between eight and nine o'clock in the evening," he replies. "And at what hour will it close?" the father asks.

"They tell me," the son answers, "that they will probably go home between two and three o'clock in the morning."

"I suppose that wine will be circulated very freely on the occasion; will it not, my son?"

"Why, yes, sir; I suppose so; but I hope that I have resolution enough not to be guilty of any excess."

"I trust that you have, my son. But do you know of any who are going to the ball who have the reputation of being intemperate?"

"Yes, sir; there will be several there who are known to drink too much wine."

"Will there be many present who are considered generally dissolute in their habits; so much so that you would not like to have them for your acquaintances?"

"There will be some such, sir, I suppose."

"It is rather dangerous," the father rejoins, "for a young man to be thrown into such company, in the midst of all the excitements of music, and dancing, and wine. It will not be easy to shake off acquaintances you may necessarily form there.

"I suppose, of course, too," adds the father, "that they have cardplaying in some of the rooms."

"Yes, sir."

"Do they play for money?"

"Some of them I believe do, sir, for small sums."

"It is not uncommon," the father replies, "under such circumstances, for persons to commence with small sums and go on to greater. Under the stimulus of play and wine, they plunge deeper and deeper into the game, till the dawn of morning finds them still with the cards in their hands. Many a young man in these scenes, commences the road to ruin. I have in my experience known a great number thus lost to virtue, and who have brought hopeless shame upon their parents and friends.

"You say, my son, that the ball will break up about three o'clock in the morning. You can, perhaps, get home and to your bed at halfpast three. You must rise at six o'clock in the morning to get the store opened in season. This allows you two hours and a half for sleep —sleep which, from the previous excitement must be feverish and un-refreshing.

"I counsel you therefore, my son," the father continues, "not to go. By going into such scenes you will be exposed to many temptations— the excitement of wine—the excitement of many dangerous passions. You can hardly avoid forming many very undesirable acquaintances. You will be invited to the gaming-table, and may thus commence the acquisition of a taste for all the excitements of gambling.

"Many may be there, who, having no pleasures except those of fashionable dissipation, will be glad to secure you as an associate.

Invitations will multiply upon you. When a young man once enters this vortex, it is difficult to get out again. When you go to the store in the morning, you will be languid and spiritless; all your energies will be exhausted. With aching head, and bloodshot eyes, and trembling limbs, you will have a day of mental depression, which will much more than counterbalance all the enjoyment of the night, and which will greatly disqualify you from discharging your duty to your employers.

"It is for these reasons," the father continues," that your parents are unwilling to have you enter such scenes. We are satisfied that, on the whole, instead of increasing, they greatly diminish, the amount of human happiness. It is on this account that we have always been desirous that neither you nor your sisters should acquire a taste for these pleasures; for our own observation, as well as the testimony of the wise and the good in all ages, has taught us that these amusements, by breaking in upon the regular and peaceful enjoyment of domestic life, expose those who engage in them to great temptation, and by prematurely exhausting the mental and bodily powers, and undermining the constitution, seriously interfere with future happiness, and lead to imminent danger.

"And when our neighbors have wondered that we should so carefully keep you away from such scenes of gaiety—from amusements which to them appeared innocent and pleasing—we have replied, that it was our conviction, that we could make you far happier by cultivating in your heart a taste for a totally different class of pleasures.

"Such pleasures, too, always leave a sting behind them. Discontent and .dissatisfaction always take possession of the soul, after a scene of unseasonable and excessive gaiety. This is always the case, in all ranks and conditions of life. Madame de Genlis, who moved in the highest circles of Parisian life, and was familiar with the gayeties of the Palais Royal, in the highest of its splendor, remarked that the days which succeeded brilliant entertainments were always melancholy.

"Therefore, my son," the father continues, "I counsel you not to go. Persevere in the plan of life which you have heretofore laid down for yourself. Come home, and spend the evening in quiet enjoyment with your mother, or your sisters; or by the perusal of some interesting volume from the library, acquire a taste for reading, and store your mind with useful knowledge. At your usual hour retire to rest. You will then rise in the morning fresh and vigorous, and in good spirits you will go to your duties. And as you see your associate in the adjoining store, who attended the ball, dozing in dejection, and lounging the live-long day at his desk, you will be thankful that you were more wise than to sacrifice so much substantial good for a few hours of midnight merriment.

"By persevering in this course," the father continues," you will more effectually secure to yourself the confidence of business men. Your credit will be better. Your prospects in life will be better. You will soon be able to have a home of your own. You will make that home more happy. Your life will glide away with far less danger of your falling before the power of temptation; and, consequently, there will be a far brighter prospect of your enjoying eternal happiness beyond the grave."

This is, in the main, the argument upon which Christians rely, and have relied, during all past ages, against the amusements and gayeties of the world. They are fully convinced that he who acquires a taste for such pleasures, will find his earthly happiness greatly impaired, and will be exposed to temptations which will greatly endanger his eternal well-being.

I have dwelt upon this subject more fully, because the young, inexperienced in the dangers of the world, often wonder why their pious parents are so unwilling that they should acquire a fondness for amusements which appear so innocent and pleasing. But I think that any ingenuous boy or girl, of fourteen or fifteen years of age, may see the force of the above considerations, and may be satisfied that Christians have not, in their decision upon this subject, acted without good reasons.

And here I do not intend to enter into the question whether these amusements might not be so far improved and refined as to obviate all objections against them. I wish to refer to them as they now are, and as they ever have been, and as there is every prospect that they will continue to be.

They are all of the same general character, leading to peculiar temptations, from the indulgence of bad passions, and the exposure of those who engage in them to unworthy associates. They all tend to destroy the taste for those quiet, domestic enjoyments, which, when cultivated, grow brighter and brighter every year, and which confer increasing solace and joy when youth has fled, and old age, and sickness, and misfortune come. Christian parents endeavor to guard their children against acquiring a taste for these pleasures, because they foresee that these amusements will, in the end, disappoint them; and they can lead them in a safer path, and one infinitely more promotive of their happiness.

We have contemplated the influence of one of these scenes of gaiety upon a young man. Let us now consider its effects upon a mother of a family, or a young lady.

In the first place in the mere preparation for any assembly of worldly gaiety and dissipation, many hours are taken from the peaceful routine of ordinary duties, in devotion to dress. Then the temptation is almost irresistible, from the strong rivalry which is called into exercise, to make expenditures which cannot well be afforded. And then, when the midnight scene of gaiety is at its height, and music's voluptuous swell is loudest, and the smile on every cheek is least clouded, how many secret sources of chagrin are necessarily fostered, though studiously concealed!

The spirit of the occasion has the strongest tendency to call into exercise the passions of envy and rivalry. The superior dress of one lady, the superior beauty of another, the comparative neglect with which one is treated, and the excessive attention which another receives, constitute the most fruitful source of vanity, on the one side, and of heart-burnings and mortifications on the other. The very nature of the enjoyment, and the whole spirit of the occasion, have the most direct tendency to call these feelings into active exercise. There is no place in which the uncomfortable feelings of the heart are so frequently and so painfully excited, as in gay, glittering assemblies. To use the familiar language of the poet,

"Though the cheek may be tinged with a warm, sunny smile, The cold heart to ruin runs on darkly the while."

And when, long after midnight, fevered with the heated room and the exciting exercise, a mother or her daughter returns to her home, how poorly is she prepared for the duties of devotion! In how unsuitable a frame of mind is she, acceptably to commune with God, and to commend herself anew, with an affectionate and a humble heart, to his service.

And then when another morning dawns, all the concerns of the family are in disorder. At a late hour she rises unrefreshed from her pillow. During the whole day she feels depressed in spirits, and unable to engage, with any satisfaction, in life's ordinary duties. It often requires one or two days of languor and dejection for the system to recover its tone, from the exhaustion of the few hours of midnight revelry. Even allowing the pleasurable emotions of the convivial hours to be as great as anyone will venture to estimate them, the enjoyment must be considered as far more than counterbalanced by the physical and intellectual reaction which necessarily ensues.

And when we go a little farther; when we consider the inevitable termination of this life of pleasure; when we contemplate the victim—for victim we must consider her—of a gay and fashionable life, after having passed through the period of youth and vigor, with her susceptibilities to these excitements worn out—her mind and heart satiated with those pursuits, and yet with no taste formed for more solid and satisfying joys—we regard her with the deepest commiseration, as an impressive warning for all the young to avoid those quicksands, upon which her happiness has been so fatally stranded.

When we turn to the Bible, to the character of our Savior and his apostles, we find these views confirmed even by the weight of inspiration; so much so, indeed, that even the idea of our Savior, or the apostle Paul, taking an active part in such scenes, is so shocking to our feelings, that the very supposition is almost irreverent. And why is it that one shrinks from such an idea, but because the spirit of the Bible is so diametrically opposed to these amusements, that the mind recoils from the thought of connecting them with sacred personages? And when we inquire of human testimony, we hear but one voice, which comes down from all past time, and from every nation, in attestation of the folly of a life of pleasure.

There are thousands now in our churches, who were once the devotees of gaiety; and they will tell you, without a contradicting voice, that, since they have abandoned their former pursuits, and sought happiness in different objects, and cultivated a taste for different pleasures, they have found peace and satisfaction, which they never knew before; and they have no more disposition to turn back to these gayeties, than they have to resume the rattles of babyhood.

It is quite important that the young should understand the true reason of the decision, to which Christians have come upon this subject. It is not a gloomy and morose spirit that dictates this decision, or any desire to prohibit real pleasures. But we see that these gayeties are, in the end, promotive of far more sorrow than happiness, and therefore we wish all whom we love, to walk in those ways of wisdom, which are pleasantness, and in those paths which are peace.

And hence, if parents would, in their own lives and in the lives of their children, bring forth the peaceable and joyful fruits of righteousness, they must avoid these scenes of gaiety. You must carefully guard against cultivating a taste for such pleasures. There are, in this world, many regions of enjoyment, where one may walk in safety. There are many joys which are improving to the heart, and which afford increasing happiness amid the infirmities of old age and approaching death—joys which, in the morning of life, are like the morning sunshine, and, in the evening of our days, are like the serene and golden hues of a summer sunset.

There are the joys of well-cultivated affections, of an improving mind, of friends, and love of home, of social converse at the quiet fireside, of the flower-garden, of the domestic animal feeding from the hand it loves, of the twilight walk in solitude or company, of visiting the sick, and cheering the desponding. There are enough sources of enjoyment which God has opened to us in this world, which are purifying in their nature, and which leave no sting behind. It is not necessary for us to search for happiness in dangerous and forbidden paths.

In all the ways pointed out in this chapter, the mother must endeavor to train up her children in the service of God. These are the practical duties of Christianity—duties which bring with them their own reward. There is no other path to heaven than that which is here pointed out—reliance upon an atoning Savior for the forgiveness of past sin, and faithful endeavors to live a devout and holy life. They who will diligently and faithfully pursue such a course, will find the Savior's yoke indeed easy, and his burden light. Duty will continually become more easy and more pleasant. The propensities and passions, whose unrestrained dominion so often mar the peace of others, will cease to trouble them—being subdued by divine grace—and they will go on their way rejoicing to the end.

# 11

# Results

FREQUENT allusion has been made in the preceding chapters, to the fatal consequences which must attend the neglect of duty. In view of this, some parents may have been oppressed and dejected. It is most surely true that the misconduct of children subjects the parents to the utmost intensity of suffering. But it must be remembered, that when parental faithfulness is attended with its usual blessing, joys, nearer akin to those of heaven than of earth, are the result. The human heart is not susceptible of more exquisite pleasures than the parental relation affords. Is there no joy when the mother first presses her infant to her heart? Is there no delight in witnessing the first placid smile which plays upon its cheek? Yes! The very earliest infancy of the babe brings "rapture a mother only knows."

## The Joy of Parenting

The very care is a delight. And when your little son has passed through the dreamy existence of infancy, and is buoyant with the activity and animated with the intelligence of childhood, are not new sources of pleasure opened to your mind? Are there no thrilling emotions of enjoyment in hearing the hearty laugh of your happy boy; in witnessing the unfolding of his active mind; in feeling his warm kiss and ardent embrace? Is there no delight in seeing your boy run to meet you, with his face full of smiles and his heart full of love; and in hearing him, in lisping accents, call you mother? As you receive daily new proofs of his affection and obedience, and see that his little bosom is animated with a generous and a noble spirit, you feel repaid an hundred fold for all your pain, anxiety, and toil.

After a few years your children arrive at maturity, and with that divine blessing which we may expect to accompany our prayerful efforts, they will be found with generous affections and established principles of piety. With what emotions do parents then look around upon their happy and prosperous family! They are receiving the earthly recompense of reward. What an affecting sight it is, to see an aged and widowed mother leaning upon the firm arm of her son, as he accompanies her to the house of God! And how many parents have had their declining years cheered by the affectionate attentions of a daughter!

Who will so tenderly watch over you in sickness as a daughter, whose bosom is animated by the principles of piety which you have inculcated? Among the sweetest earthly joys to be experienced in old age, is the joy of looking around upon happy and grateful children. The marks of esteem and love that you receive from them, will daily be rewarding you for all your toil. And when your children's children cluster around you, giving unceasing tokens of respect and affection, you will find in their caresses the renewal of your youth. When all other earthly joys have faded, you will find in the little prattlers of the fireside untiring enjoyment.

But there is a scene of still brighter happiness. The Christian family will meet again. Parents and children will be associated in heaven. And when the whole household are happily assembled there; when they sit down together in the green pastures and by the still waters; when they go in and out at the mansions which God has prepared for them; then, and not till then, will they experience the fullness of the enjoyment with which God rewards parental fidelity. How full of rapture is the thought that the whole family may meet again in the world of songs and everlasting joy, where sorrow and sighing shall forever flee away!

As from that happy state of existence you look back upon your pilgrimage on earth, you can never regret any labor that you have expended, any sacrifices that you have made, any sufferings that you have undergone, to train up your children to be with you the heirs of a glorious immortality. O, there is enough, abundantly enough, to encourage every parent to unwearied exertions! As with the deep emotions of parental love, you look upon the obedient and affectionate children who surround your fireside, your thoughts may be carried away to enjoyments infinitely richer, and forever enduring, in the world to come.

We may be called upon to follow our children to the grave. And heart-rending is such an affliction. But if we have reason to believe that they will go to the mansions which the Savior has prepared, much of the bitterness of the affliction is taken away. There cares and trials have ended. They are sheltered from every storm. They are protected from every sorrow. Soaring in angelic flights, and animated with celestial joys, we and our young ones will be welcomed by God, at such time when he shall give us entrance to those happy worlds. A gentleman was once asked if he had lost any of his children. "No," he replied, "There are two I won't see until heaven, but have lost none." To a truly Christian family the death of anyone of its members is but a temporary absence, and not an eternal separation.

## A Powerful Influence

The influence of mothers has as powerful an action upon the welfare of future generations, as all other earthly causes combined. Thus far the history of the world has been composed of the narrations of oppression and blood. War has scattered its unnumbered woes. The cry of the oppressed has unceasingly ascended to heaven. Where are we to look for the influence which shall change this scene, and fill the earth with the fruits of peace and benevolence? It is to the power of divine truth, to Christianity, as taught from a mother's lips. In a vast majority of cases the first six or seven years of life decide the character of the man. If the boy leave the paternal roof uncontrolled, turbulent, and vicious, he will, in all probability, rush on in the mad career of self-indulgence.

There are exceptions; but these exceptions are rare. If, on the other hand, your son goes from home accustomed to control himself, he will probably retain that habit through life. If he has been taught to make sacrifices of his own enjoyment that he may promote the happiness of those around him, it may be expected that he will continue to practice benevolence, and consequently will be respected, and useful, and happy. If he has adopted firm resolutions to be faithful in all the relations of life, he, in all probability, will be a virtuous man and an estimable citizen, and a benefactor of his race.

When our land is filled with pious and patriotic mothers, then will it be filled with virtuous and patriotic men. The world's redeeming influence, under the blessing of the Holy Spirit, must come from a mother's lips. She who was first in the transgression, must be yet the principal earthly instrument in the restoration. Other causes may greatly aid. Other influences must be ready to receive the mind as it comes from the mother's hand, and carry it onward in its improvement. But the mothers of our race must be the chief instruments in its redemption. This sentiment will bear examining; and the more it is examined, the more manifestly true will it appear. It is alike the dictate of philosophy and experience. The mother who is neglecting personal effort, and relying upon other influences for the formation of virtuous character in her children, will find, when it is too late, that she has fatally erred.

The patriot, who hopes that schools, and lyceums, and the general diffusion of knowledge, will promote the good order and happiness of the community, while family government is neglected, will find that he is attempting to purify the streams which are flowing from a corrupt fountain. It is maternal influence, after all, which must be the great agent, in the hands of God, in bringing back our guilty race to duty and happiness. O that mothers could feel this responsibility as they ought! Then would the world assume a different aspect. Then should we less frequently behold unhappy families and broken-hearted parents. A new race of men would enter upon the busy scene of life, and cruelty and crime would pass away. O mothers! reflect upon the power which your Maker has placed in your hands! There is no earthly influence to be compared with yours. There is no combination of causes so powerful in promoting the happiness or the misery of our race, as the instructions of home. In a most peculiar sense God has constituted you the guardians and the controllers of the human family.

## The Involvement of Fathers

Perhaps someone asks, "Is there nothing for the fathers to do?" There certainly is much—very much. But this treatise is prepared to impress upon the mind the duties of mothers. Yet, lest it should be inferred from what has been written, that the whole duty of family government rests upon the mother, I would briefly remark, that no father can be justified in releasing himself from a full share of the responsibility. A father will often make many excuses to release himself from his duty; but alas! he cannot release his children from the ruin, or himself from the woe, which his neglect occasions. It will be a poor solace to him, as he goes in shame and sorrow to the grave, to reflect that he was busily engaged in other employments while leaving his children to mature for ignominy and disgrace. What duties can be paramount to those which we owe to our children?

A clergyman sometimes says he has so much to do, his time is so fully occupied, that he is compelled to neglect his children. And who has the first claim upon his-attention, his congregation or his children? God has placed him over a congregation, and has also made him the father of a family, and which duty does God regard as most imperative? And yet not a few instances might be pointed out, in which clergymen of devoted piety and extensive usefulness, have given their whole attention to the labors of the study and to public duties, and have left their unhappy children to grow up unchecked and vicious. No one can enjoy the privilege of being a father, without having duties to perform which will require time and care. And can any time be more usefully employed than that which is passed in training up a family of children, who shall remain to do good in the world long after we are silent in the grave?

Can we have any influence equal to that of pious sons and daughters? Can we bequeath to the world a richer legacy than the fervent piety and active usefulness of a numerous offspring? O there is no sin which reaches so far, and extends such wide-spreading desolation, as parental neglect. No father can be guiltless in retiring from these responsibilities. The first duty enjoined upon us, is to keep our own hearts with diligence; the second, to lead our families to God; the third, to consult for the spiritual welfare of our neighbors; the fourth, to do all in our power to evangelize the world. And yet how many Christian ministers have paralyzed their influence, destroyed their peace of mind, and broken their hearts, by neglecting the duties which they owe to their children.

Many of the most eminent statesmen of the land are thus afflicted and dishonored. And the affliction must be aggravated by the consciousness that they are reaping as they have sown. I would not willingly inflict a pang upon the heart of any parent who reads these pages, but I cannot refrain from raising a warning voice, in view of the destruction which has gone forth, and is still going forth; from the cause we are now contemplating. The temptation is very great, for men who are engaged in literary pursuits, or overwhelmed with public cares, to neglect their domestic duties. But how ruinous is this to usefulness and happiness.

It is better to be a poor man, and it is better to be a humble man, than to be disgraced in life by the profligacy of those who call us father, and to have a dying pillow planted with thorns by our children's hands. Every man, whatever be his situation in life, is bound to regard the duties which he owes to his children as among the most sacred that he has to discharge. If he neglects them, he must reap the bitter consequences.

One other remark I must here make, as it is intimately connected with a mother's duty. A father should always endeavor to teach his children to honor their mother. If the father does not do this, the difficulties of the mother will be vastly increased. But where harmony of design is seen to exist between the parents, authority is strengthened. There is something in loving and revering a mother, which exerts a delightful influence upon the heart; it refines and elevates the character; and is a strong safeguard against degrading vice. Boys in particular will not long respect a mother, if they see that their father does not treat her with attention.

You can hardly find a dissolute young man, who has been accustomed from infancy to look to his mother with respect and love. It is in disobedience to a mother that the career of crime generally commences. The way is thus prepared for the disregard of all parental authority. And then the progress is rapid to the boldest defiance of all the laws of God and man. Many an unhappy criminal has, from the gallows, traced back his course of guilt to the early periods of childhood, when he commenced with disobedience to a mother's commands; and he has felt and acknowledged that, had he then been habituated to obey them, his whole succeeding course had probably been different. It is therefore of the first importance that nothing should be omitted tending to give the mother great and unceasing influence over the minds of her children.

## The Benefits of Education

The subject of education must be attended to with persevering study. And yet how many parents neglect this duty! Nothing surely can be of greater importance to the parents and child, than a correct system of family government. Every mother admits her need of information. There are many valuable books, easy of access, which will afford great assistance. A mother should consider it one of her first duties to inform herself upon this subject, as far as her means will admit. The art of influencing and guiding the youthful mind, is susceptible of almost boundless improvement, and we are unfaithful to our children if we do not become familiar with the results of the experiments of others.

We ought not to stumble in darkness, when light is shining around us. There are fundamental principles in operating upon the human mind, as well as in any other science. And many an anxious mother has fallen into error, to the serious injury of her children, which she might have avoided, had she consulted the sources of information which are at everyone's hand.

How great must be the affliction of that mother, who, in consequence of neglect, has been unsuccessful with her family! She looks upon her ruined sons, and reproaches herself with the just reflection, that if she had pursued a different course, they might have been her joy and blessing. Perhaps even they throw reproaches upon her, and attribute all their guilt and wretchedness to her bad government. But few more miserable men have passed through the world than Lord Byron; and he has distinctly attributed the formation of his character, and, consequently all his crime and woe, to his mother's unrestrained passions, and neglect of proper government.

How must such a crimination from a dissolute son, pierce the heart of a pious mother! Knowledge of duty might have been attained, but she neglected to attain it, and through inexcusable ignorance ruined her child. An affectionate mother would be overwhelmed with anguish, if she had ignorantly administered some poisonous drug to her child, and had seen him in consequence expiring in agony. But how much more dreadful is it to see moral ruin caused by our own criminal ignorance! Who would not rather see a son or a daughter lie down in the grave, than see them sink into the wretchedness and disgrace of profligacy. If we would save our children then we must be earnest and faithful in our duty.

www.ingramcontent.com/pod-product-compliance
Lightning Source LLC
Chambersburg PA
CBHW070100080526
44586CB00013B/1141